An A
For All

CW01475581

An Angler
For All Seasons

the best of
H. T. Sheringham

Chosen and Introduced by Tom Fort

Wood Engravings by Chris Wormell

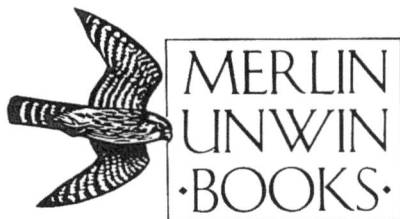

MERLIN
UNWIN
·BOOKS·

Contents

Acknowledgements

The essays by H. T. Sheringham which are reproduced in this anthology have previously appeared in the following publications:

An Open Creel, first published by Methuen in 1910
An Angler For All Seasons chapters: 1, 4, 5, 9, 10, 14, 15, 17, 18

Trout Fishing Memories and Morals, first published by Hodder & Stoughton in 1920
An Angler For All Seasons chapters: 6, 8, 16

An Anglers Hours, first published by MacMillan in 1905
An Angler For All Seasons chapters: 7, 12, 19, 20, 23

Coarse Fishing, first published by A&C Black in 1912
An Angler For All Seasons chapter 13

The Field magazine, January 1921, February 1921, July 1921, November 1919
An Angler For All Seasons chapters: 2, 3, 11, 21, 22

Journal of the Flyfishers' Club, summer 1916
An Angler For All Seasons chapter 24

The publishers wish to express their particular thanks to *The Field* and The Flyfishers' Club for their co-operation, and to Tom Fort, journalist for the *Financial Times*, for his help in putting together this anthology.

Introduction

BY TOM FORT

It was a little over a quarter of a century ago that my eyes were first opened to the possibility that there might be more to fishing than catching - or, more commonly in my own distressing case, failing to catch - fish. One of my elder brothers and I, browsing in a second-hand bookshop in Reading, came upon a case of books on angling. We were passionate fishermen, but of a severely non-spiritual kind and this was reflected in the few books we then possessed. I remember a volume called *Coarse Fishing With The Experts* and a series of little manuals on catching perch and roach and the like.

Among the books we bought that day was one bound in faded red cloth. Its spine was decorated with two crossed fishing rods, between which were a net and a fat basket with lid raised to display something resembling a chub or carp. It cost two and sixpence and was called *An Open Creel*. The author's name, H. T. Sheringham, was as it happened, faintly familiar to us. For, in addition to our handful of practical treatises, we did have another book - BB's *Confessions of a Carpfisher*, which includes an immortal account of a battle royal with a big carp at Cheshunt Reservoir written by this selfsame Sheringham.

I read *An Open Creel* straight through, with a swiftly swelling sense of wonder and delight. Even now, I can recall the condition of hilarity to which I was reduced by the chapter entitled 'A Day of Tribulation', in which Sheringham describes a succession of calamities which overtook him during a day's wet fly fishing, presumably on the Exe near Dulverton.

I was, at that time, making my own first, cack-handed attempts to educate myself in the use of a fly rod. It was a great solace to find the despair, which unfailingly overwhelmed me as I sought to deliver my flies in the teeth of gales, mirrored in this light-footed but deeply felt prose. Just as I had railed against a cruelly indifferent Providence, so Sheringham - having left his cast in a bush over deep water - sat down to contrast his misfortunes with those of Job. A little while later came the loss of the big fish on which his heart was set, 'leaving me to my thoughts of Job and his exaggerated griefs.'

In his introduction to *An Open Creel*, Sheringham refers in characteristic fashion to its predecessor, *An Angler's Hours*, which had been published five years earlier in 1905. 'There was about that volume,' he writes, 'a certain smugness; in nearly all its chapters fish were slain and weighed and reckoned up and made the object of fat complacency.' He declares his intention to offer a more balanced picture of the sport, to lift the veil on the angler's sorrows in order to tell a little of those days which end with the creel lamentably empty.

For myself, I had no creel. But if I had had one, its customary condition would, indeed, have been one of lamentable emptiness, for I was a most incompetent fisherman. At once, I felt that this man was talking to me.

I should complete the story of my discovery of H. T. Sheringham. Having devoured *An Open Creel*, my brothers and I (for a third also became a devotee) rushed back to the shop in Reading and snapped up *Elements of Angling* (first published in 1908) and *Coarse Fishing* (1912). These are both works of instruction and much of the content is, inevitably, dated. But each is beautifully written, awash with humour and good sense and well worth the effort of tracking down. They also illustrate a central - and for me most endearing - aspect of Sheringham's angling philosophy: his passion for the so-called coarse fishes. I shall return to this subject later.

There were no more Sheringhams in the Reading book shop. But by now the fire of our enthusiasm was lit and we wasted no time in obtaining *Trout Fishing: Memories and Morals* from a dealer (alas, at a dealer's price). *An Angler's Hours* took a little more hunting down, but with that the Sheringham oeuvre was almost complete (I exclude his *Fishing: Its Cause, Treatment and Cure*, a slight and overtly humorous book which he published in the 1920s; and also a handful of novels, among them *Syllabub Farm*). This burst of buying laid the foundations of our collection of fishing books, and sowed the seeds of an acquisitive appetite still unsatisfied today.

I now have custody of most of the books, almost six hundred of them. I cherish them all, even the ones I have never got round to reading. And there are writers to whom I return again and again: J. W. Hills, Zane Grey, Roderick Haig-Brown, BB, G. D. Luard, Frank Barker, F. A. Mitchell-Hedges, Richard Walker, Chris Yates, Negley Farson, Stephen Johnson, Arthur Ransome, Harry Plunket Greene. All of them I regard as friends, and all of them I admire for the way they have brought the sport to life. Yet, for all the hundreds of fishing books I have read since those distant days of enlightenment, I have never had occasion to change the opinion I must have formed then: that Hugh Tempest Sheringham was the finest of them all.

The Sheringhams were a family of strong clerical leanings. Hugh Sheringham was brought up in Tewkesbury, where his father was Vicar. His grandfather had been Archdeacon of Gloucester. Sheringham himself rebelled against this affinity for the Church. His son John (to whom I am grateful for much biographical and personal detail) remembers him as a convinced atheist, although - as a consequence of his great love of singing - he remained a devoted member of the church choir in the Oxfordshire village of Eynsham, where he made his home for the last ten years of his life.

The flavour of his childhood and the dawning of the passion for rivers, are exquisitely captured in the opening chapter of *An Open Creel*, 'Waters of Youth'. The affection for the chub - whether caught on worm or cheese or, best of all, fly - was born on the Severn and Avon and their tributaries and was never to leave him. While his grandfather, the stern Archdeacon, endeavoured to bend him to the discipline of Latin verse, the boy's imagination ran on water meadows, the play of sunlight on moving water, the tantalising mysteries of the depths beneath the hanging branches of willows. But the young Sheringham was a gifted scholar and that strict classical education - apart from leaving him with a sometimes excessive affection for Latin tags - was to stand him in good stead when it came to developing his graceful, easy style of writing.

He won a scholarship to Westminster and took a classical tripos at Cambridge. This was followed by a year in Germany, where he mixed study with amusement and enjoyed, on an unnamed river, what was numerically the greatest catch of his life - seventy-two trout. 'It was a great day, certainly,' he recalled later. 'But it did not seem like fishing. It was more like gathering in the harvest.'

The Sheringhams were undoubtedly of the gentry, but neither moneyed nor landed. After the carefree student days, circumstances dictated that Hugh Sheringham should earn a living. The meeting which was to seal his fate occurred beside that most lovely Berkshire chalkstream, the Lambourn. In his fishing diary - kindly lent to me by Justin Knowles, the founder of the Flyfisher's Classic Library - Sheringham recorded the event tersely:

'September 1903. Spent three weeks at Newbury, principally on the Lambourn. Caught many trout, but only about three brace of grayling the whole time. Met W.S. there, and so appointed to *The Field*.'

W. S. was William Senior, then editor of *The Field* and well known as the author of a number of fishing books published under the pseudonym Red Spinner. Sheringham was then just short of his 27th birthday and he was to remain Angling Editor of *The Field* until his death, 27 years later. As enthusiasts for fishing literature, I suppose we should be grateful for the fact that he made journalism his career. Had he gone into the Church, or the diplomatic service, or to the British Museum - which was apparently his ambition - he might well have joined the great throng of us whose immortal masterpieces remain firmly locked inside our heads.

As it was, by subjecting himself to the constant, nagging demands of journalism, he produced a mass of writing which made him among the most cherished and respected authorities on fishing of his day. What is more, in his role as an editor, he encouraged, cajoled, flattered and browbeat a host of friends, acquaintances and complete strangers into putting pen to paper. Harry Plunket Greene's *Where the Bright Waters Meet* is merely the most celebrated of the books to which Sheringham acted as midwife.

Yet there was, I suspect, a sadness in this working life. John Sheringham believes that his father regarded himself as a partial failure; that he reproached himself for not having made better use of his talents. Though he must have enjoyed the writing of many of those inimitable articles and the experiences on which they were based, there must also have been much that was oppressive drudgery - in particular, in the immense annual labour of producing the guide, *Where to Fish*.

There were disappointments, too. One was being passed over for the editorship of *The Field*. Another - according to Sheringham's brother-in-law, H. D. Turing - was the comparatively poor sales achieved by *Trout Fishing: Memories And Morals*. This was published in 1920 and was regarded by Sheringham as embodying much of his angling creed. But in the depressed post-war years, it did nothing like as well as the earlier books.

From this point onwards, Sheringham's energy and appetite for writing declined. His essays in *The Field* became few and far between as the 1920s progressed, until they ceased almost completely. Nor - apart from *Fishing: Its Cause, Treatment and Cure* - were there to be any more fishing books. In addition, he was dogged by worries about money and, increasingly, by ill-health. His son recalls an atmosphere of chronic indigence prevailing at the family home in Eynsham. It was a condition not assisted by Sheringham's notorious unworldliness, reflected in the fact that, at a time of particular penury, no less than three men were being employed to tend the garden. There is a poignant entry in the diary for 1923, recording Sheringham's resignation from the local club which had the fishing on the Windrush, on the grounds of expense.

During the war, Sheringham was head of the editorial department at the Ministry of Information and seems to have suffered some sort of breakdown as a result of overwork. Several of the tributes to him on his death refer to the change in him which his friends observed when he returned to *The Field* in 1918. He began to suffer attacks, apparently of epilepsy, which caused giddiness, severe headaches and loss of memory. There are several entries in the diary which refer to these attacks, more than one of which occurred when he was fishing the Houghton Club water on the Test. Although 1930 seemed to bring an improvement in his health, it was temporary and he died of cancer in December 1930 - 'peacefully,' wrote H. D. Turing, 'at the first hint of dawn.'

As well as being an atheist, H. T. Sheringham was a socialist. It was a combination which, at that time, was a little more unusual among members of his class than it was later to become. One of the few distinct memories that his son John has of his father is of an opera staged in the garden at Eynsham, with proceeds going to the Labour Party (another is of being beaten by HTS for kicking a cat). It may sound far-fetched to argue that Sheringham applied socialism to fishing, but it seems to have been the case. His friend John Moore - with whom he collaborated on editing the *The Book Of The Fly Rod* - wrote: 'It was chiefly the humbler angler that he loved and by whom he was loved in return. He always preferred that a river should be bought by a large angling club than by a single millionaire or a syndicate of plutocrats.'

Although Sheringham clearly relished his days on preserved stretches of the Itchen, Test or Kennet, he always fished them as a guest and was never to be counted a member of a syndicate of plutocrats. The kind of fishing club he liked was the one he celebrated in 'A Suburban Fishery', in *An Angler's Hours*, where a man might stalk a trout or two, then cast a fly for chub and finish his day watching his float circle a shaded eddy in the hope that the perch or roach might bite.

It was in his passion for coarse fishing that what one might term Sheringham's democratic instincts are most apparent. He wrote in his introduction to *Coarse Fishing*: 'Salmon-fishing is good; trout fishing is good; but to the complete angler neither is intrinsically better than the pursuit of roach, or tench, or perch, or pike.' Put like that, it sounds so reasonable.

Yet, coming from a man of Sheringham's social background, this creed was almost heretical. Men like Halford did not demean themselves by considering the ways of chub. Only the salmon in his Scottish torrent and the noble trout of the chalkstream, were considered worthy of a gentleman's time and study. Sheringham's partiality for floats and spinners, worms and cheese, an 18-foot rod and a Nottingham-style centrepin reel, made him an object of curiosity among his friends. Plunket Greene, for instance, portrays him as 'diggling for sticklebacks,' and 'sitting in a punt watching a float for hours at a time on the chance of flicking a two-inch pinkeen over his shoulder.'

As a trout fisherman, he was clearly no mean performer and he was as thrilled as the next man by a great hatch of blue-winged olives on the Test, or the spectacle of mighty Kennet trout gorging themselves on the mayfly. But he seems to have been happier still battling his way up some inconsequential and overgrown brook or weed-choked carrier, employing every conceivable minor tactic to winkle out a brace or two of wild, wary trout.

He loved rivers like the lower Kennet, the Colne and the Evenlode, where democracy reigned and the fish which rose to his fly was as likely to be a chub or a dace as a trout. As for salmon, he caught his share, mainly from the Welsh Dee and the Coquet in Northumberland. But he maintained an air of lofty indifference to the celebrated, exclusive rivers of Scotland and appears to have believed that those who fished them and nowhere else, were not truly to be counted of the brotherhood.

He was, by all accounts, a gentle and most lovable man. His friends prized him for the humour of his conversation, his scholarship, his immense knowledge of angling's traditions and literature; for his insistence on being supplied with afternoon tea; for his ability to conjure a brace from an improbable spot on an impossible day. Above all, he inspired through his writing respect and affection from friends and unknown subscribers alike. In his heyday, before the Great War, there was only one question to be asked on the day *The Field* came out; 'Has HTS anything in this week?'

H. D. Turing deftly identified the nature of Sheringham's originality as a writer on fishing. Before him there were, broadly speaking, two mainstream styles in angling writing. One - exemplified by Halford - was that of the teacher addressing his pupils, a colossus condescending to instruct mere mortals. The other - with a deplorable tendency towards the sentimental, contrived and verbose - sustained the fiction that the capture of a fish was of no consequence at all, compared with the ecstasy derived from a communion with nature as found on the river bank.

Sheringham's voice came as a fresh breeze, dispersing the tired old conventions. He spoke of fishing as other fishermen found it, of rare triumphs and frequent reverses, of the joy of escape which is at the heart of the sport's attraction. He subscribed whole heartedly to the axiom that it is better to catch fish than not to do so - but knew well enough that, for ordinary folk, success in fishing as in other matters could never easily be won. He defined the angler's season thus: 'Of the total number of his days, probably two-thirds will give him no results worth mentioning. Three-quarters of the rest will be of the type conveniently labelled "fair to middling". And there may be two or three days of really fine sport, days about which he at once writes articles. An article or two may be written about days of the second class, but about those of the first there is a grim silence.'

He broke that grim silence and also left an incomparable record of those days of the second class. He did not preach from some mountain top, compelling an envious awe for his fishcatching expertise; but spoke to his fellows as an equal. And he did so in a manner at once wise, humorous, unaffected, fresh and elegant.

The curious thing is that I feel I have known him for a long time - almost, that I have fished with him. He lived for several years in a house not more than a couple of miles from my own. From his diary I have learned that he fished the same Kennet millpool, which is now my favourite haunt when the mood is on me for a couple of hours, after chub or barbel. Ever since I first read the books, I have enjoyed his company - as Eric Parker described him 'an angler gay and wise, an eager comrade, humorous scholar, truthful and loyal friend.' My hope in presenting this anthology is that more of the brotherhood may make and enjoy, his acquaintance.

Tom Fort, Burghfield Common, April 1992.

CHAPTER ONE

Waters of Youth

The other day, while turning out some old papers by way of making the new year less crowded than its predecessor, I came upon a faded old photograph of a group of young people seated and standing in the constrained fashion of those who are being sacrificed to the amateur camera. One peculiarly villainous countenance purports to be my own, and I should not be too zealous to acknowledge the impeachment were it not for a certain far-away look in the eyes which has reminded me of something. I remember now that I was looking through the leafless trees at a glint of water, and wondering whether the three roach would live or die. In moments of crisis, such as are caused by the dentist's chair or the uncovered lens, one has these flashes of disconnected thought.

The three roach, as a matter of fact, were in the water, a small pond between the garden and the stable-yard, and I had put them there that morning just before luncheon. They came from a little river about half a mile away, and were the trophies of my angle, brought home in a landing-net to convince certain scoffers (the photograph punishes them enough) who said that no man could catch fish in the little river during the winter, because when earth is bound in frost-chains fishes burrow into the mud, and are no more seen. In those days my mind was by no means clear upon this point, but disagreement seemed to be expected of me, and I disagreed. More than that, I borrowed a primitive sort of rod and line from the principal scoffer, dug myself some worms, and went down the hill to the river after breakfast. The banks were hard with frost, and the edges of the stream were lined with ice, but, not a little to my surprise, I had some bites, and in a short time caught the three roach. Then I returned, cold but satisfied, to find the fish were still alive when I got back to the house. So they were turned into the pond before a company of respectful onlookers. Maybe their descendants are there yet if the pond still exists.

The discovery of the old photograph and the memory of the incident of that day have set old strings in vibration, and thoughts of other ponds belonging to a further past come up unbidden. Among them are the ponds of Arden, the fair country in which I was privileged, with a small number of other boys, to imbibe the rudiments of education. We were a lucky set of youngsters in many ways. Too few in most years to make up an eleven at cricket or football, we were allowed a great deal of liberty for other country pursuits, and we used to cover miles every afternoon in search of birds' eggs, butterflies, and other treasures, or in following the hounds, which came within reach several times every season. One thing only was not regarded with favour by the authorities, and that was fishing. I never quite understood why it was discouraged, but it was; only about once a term were we allowed to go out with the sanction of authority and angle in the little stream that ran through the village.

We always made a festival of this solemn occasion, and we nearly always caught something worth having, for we were easily satisfied. Minnows were not despised, gudgeon were greeted with rapture, and the occasional triumph of a roach, with gorgeous red eyes, was a thing beyond words. Once one of us caught a golden minnow, a very beautiful little fish such as I have never seen since, though I have heard of a specimen now and again. Most of our captures were kept alive and put into 'the pond', a funny little piece of water in the stable yard, flanked on two sides by the kitchen-garden wall, and on the third by two small willow trees. Round in shape, about twenty feet in diameter, and filled debris in the shape of old tins, sunken fragments of toy boats, bottles, and other remnants, it was by no means the place into which fish ought to have been put, for their speedy demise was practically certain. The odd thing was, however, that our fish thrived in the uncongenial puddle. They would even take a worm at times, and, in default of better occupation, we used to angle for them with withy twigs, cotton lines, and bent pins. The gudgeon adapted themselves to the pond best, but bull-heads also lived there pretty well, and also stone-loach, when we could get them home alive, which was rather difficult. One afternoon a great surprise came to us in the shape of a little carp, which must have been in the pond all the time, for none of us had put him there. He remains a mystery unsolved to this day.

There were other ponds in Arden - the stickleback pond which was within the school grounds, the newt pond in the copse where the bluebells grew, and others further afield which held genuine fish. To angle in these we had to be very subtle, and to escape the notice of the authorities in our exits and entrances. Even a telescopic Japanese rod does not look like a very convincing walking-stick, and an ordinary rod concealed partly by trousers and partly by coat must give its owner a curious gait. Perhaps the authorities winked at our *ruses innocents*, perhaps we were never discovered. At any rate, I remember no dire penalties incurred on that count, though for other offences we were rightly chastised now and then. One of the distant ponds held a species of merry little fish of a reddish-bronze colour, which we never could catch. They would come and suck at the Russian lily-leaves close by our very feet in the most impudent manner, but they would not take any kind of paste or grub or worm, at any rate with a hook in it. What they were I still do not know, but I think they may have been crucian carp.

Another pond, which was really a kind of backwater of the river, was a very thrilling place. Here we angled concealed amongst the bushes at its edge in great fear and trembling, for not only was the place forbidden by the general law of piscary, but the school authorities used often to walk this way; moreover, there was a fierce notice-board upon a neighbouring tree, and the landowner was an object of much awe to us, being an intimate friend of the authorities, and therefore, presumably, in league with them, as well as anxious to conserve his own property. These tremors gave an added zest to the occasional captures that used to reward our visits. The fish were for the most part roach, with one or two small chub. I never remember catching more than two at any one time. I grieve to say that Sunday afternoon was our favourite occasion for the foray. We presumed on the law of orthodox English nature which ordains that the forenoon of the day shall be spent in church, and the afternoon in quiet meditation on the sermon which has been preached. A least, that is my interpretation of Sunday proceedings now; in those innocent days we held that the authorities slept.

Some miles away from our school there was a lake which never ceased to rouse our curiosity and cupidity, and to the end of my life I shall remember the night when we first had ocular demonstration of its possibilities. There was a very aged person (he seemed so to us, being about eighteen) who came to read with the authorities, and to while away the time before some examination. Being so old, he was highly privileged, and to us he seemed a perfect Nimrod, for he had a gun and a real fly-rod, actually caught a trout in the little river, and even soared so high as to obtain permission to fish in the enchanted lake. And so one evening he returned with no less than eight roach which he had captured alone and unaided. They must have weighed about six ounces apiece, and spread out on rushes on a dish they made an imposing spectacle. Envy but mildly expresses my own feelings on that occasion. Not long afterwards another visit to the water had even more wonderful results, and the hero came back with two fish bigger than seemed possible. They were bream, he said, and they weighed about two and a half pounds apiece. He was good enough to reward our open-mouthed admiration with some instructions on the art of catching these leviathans. I can still remember his telling us that you had to have two rods, bait with lobworms on the bottom, and sit afar off, maintaining absolute silence until a bite came. I have a shrewd suspicion that he had learnt these facts himself for the first time that very day (from the keeper), but I may be wrong; perhaps jealousy still lingers. In those better days, though I envied, I thought no guile. The opportunity of fishing that lake never came to me at that time, but in after-years I visited it more than once. It is sad that the visits only led to a conviction that 'we are not such as we were,' and that it is unwise to seek interpretation of a happy dream.

One more pond is still vividly pictured before my eyes, and yet I only saw it twice. The authorities rode now and then to visit a clerical friend a good many miles away, and twice, on early summer afternoons, another boy and I went also on the ponies which were hired two or three times a week for our instruction in the art of riding. We thoroughly enjoyed these excursions, for the rector's cakes were of very noble quality and profusion. I was in a mood of great spiritual exaltation, after partaking thereof, when I first saw the pond, so my first impressions may have been transcendental. But undoubtedly the pond was a very lovely place. It lay at some distance from the house, and one had to jump down a ha-ha from the lawn, then crossing a park-like meadow. The water was rectangular in shape, and probably not more than fifty yards long, though to me it seemed immense. But the most noticeable thing about it, even to a small boy thinking of fish, was the magnificent display of rhododendrons, whose great green leaves and glowing petals formed almost a wall round the banks. In the gaps grew long meadow grass, and the whole scene was vivid with life, for butterflies and lesser insects were everywhere. The water was of a greenish quality and looked deep, and I remember thinking that such a big pond, with such big flowers round it, must hold very big fish. But on that occasion I saw nothing, though the reverend lord of the soil, whom, despite a cynical smile from the authorities, I ventured to question on the subject, said that there were fish there, and that I might catch them next time if I liked. I was never able to try, alas! for my horsemanship did not warrant my carrying a rod as well as a crop, but on the second visit I saw a fish. It was unlike any fish that I see nowadays, being long and green, and moving like a ghost. I have been wondering ever since what it was.

Besides these ponds, there were two brooks, feeders of the small river. One contained loaches of noble size, but very difficult to catch, because the water was rather deep. To take these agile fish in Nature's way - which was our way - one ought to be able to stand in the bed of the stream, and, stooping, to make a trap of one's two hands, into which a fish would dart when judiciously stirred from under its stone. We had not read *Lorna Doone* in those days, so the idea of a loach-spear never occurred to us.

For the bull-heads in the other brook we used not only to grope, but also to angle. Sometimes we would do it in the most barefaced manner. Raising a likely stone, we discovered our quarry lurking beneath. If the stone was then very gently replaced, the fish apparently took no alarm, and after an interval a little red worm on a small hook placed at the edge of his haunt would have the desired effect. But there was one deep pool in which we had to use a float, and from this I - no, I am not sure that it was I - we caught on a never-to-be-forgotten day a fish, a great fish, a miraculous fish, a fish with red spots. It was the first trout, and it weighed belike two ounces. We went home, 'striking the stars with our august heads.' One more trout we had out of the same brook lower down, where it was bigger, but I will not dwell on the incident. It was at the period when we collected butterflies and were never abroad without butterfly-nets.

Contemporary with the schooldays in Arden are memories of fishing in the summer holidays, all detached and fragmentary. They amount to little more than a series of mental pictures, with myself more or less heroic in the foreground - more, as when, at about the age of ten, I saw the huge perch cruising about under the camp-sheeting, seized by main force the rod of a protesting but smaller playmate, and, again by main force, hauled the fish to dry land and fell upon it. I believe it weighed one and a half pounds. The rod, a telescopic Japanese thing, was broken in the crisis, and I seem to remember that there ensued what are popularly known as 'words'. I also remember the worm which brought about that victory, a peculiarly yellow bilious-looking object. Less heroic do I appear in the picture where, eager to be after the gudgeons in the backwater, I jump incautiously into the boat alongside the landing-stage, and fall out of it on the other side. The presence of grown-up spectators, who regarded me as a heaven-sent opportunity for mirth, made the experience a bitter one. Besides, I was sent home to change, and so wasted a whole glorious hour of life.

Other pictures of early days include a bridge over a canal, under which I used to sit, heart in mouth, gazing down into the clear water at very small perch in session about my bait; and a weir-pool on the Yorkshire Derwent, where I caught gudgeon and watched an impressive figure standing on a stone near the further shore fly-fishing for, I was told, grayling. I did not know what grayling were, but I saw the flash of silver when he used his landing net, and assumed them to be a specially desirable kind of roach. One holiday was spent at Berwick-on-Tweed, and there I made the acquaintance of the 'poddler'. That sporting fellow - the young of the coalfish - became promptly the centre of existence for me. Waking or sleeping, I thought of nothing put poddlers, and was to be found at all hours of the day walking up and down the long stone pier, holding a long rod and trailing in the water the traditional tackle - three white flies, a pipe-lead, and a baby spinner - or sitting with my feet dangling over the edge, and offering pieces of herring for the consideration of any fish that cared for them.

Once I caught a large red mullet, which made me very proud. Once, too, I assisted, as spectator, in a great draught of salmon, seventy or eighty of them in the net all at once. I approved of the proceedings when the fishermen leaped into the shallow water and began to lay about them with their clubs; but otherwise I was not much interested in salmon. Poddlers were my fancy. They caused me to refuse to go to Edinburgh, Melrose, and other objects of family pilgrimage; they made me think and speak slightingly of the Whitadder, whither I was lured one day by false promises of trout; they filled me with a hatred for a certain person which I have hardly got over yet. He was about my own age, and he carried two immense ones on a string. And he refused for them three-halfpence, and a pocket-knife, and a hook! Poddlers, in fact, were the important part of Berwick-on-Tweed. They were Berwick-on-Tweed.

Some matters are there which it were well to touch on but lightly - my first catch of jack, for instance, made with a Devon minnow in April! A severe reproof by a stranger as I walked home displaying them in triumph gave me my first idea of what the close season meant. Other memories, however, are legitimate enough and very delightful. I fear I should not now find fair a certain small stream, branch of an important river, which of old gave me much thrilling sport, but in those days it was a river of Eden. Somewhere in the background of recollection is a consciousness that its bottom was principally composed of tin cans, bottles, and other contributions from a neighbouring small town; some faint echo of a whisper seems to remind me that the same town trusted largely to Providence and the flowing water for a sewage system; but in effect I do not remember these drawbacks. What I do remember is the ancient willow leaning out over the stream, and the eddy below it caused by the release of water narrowed by the willow roots. There was a blissful day when I caught four dozen roach out of that eddy and at the edge of the stream. The fish came on to feed about mid-day, and they would only take little red worms - rather an odd thing in summer. I was, of course, late for lunch and duly reprimanded, but I had such a basket of roach as no other boy took out of the stream those holidays. That the fish scarcely averaged three ounces apiece does not even now dim the glory of that achievement.

There were other triumphs connected with that mile of water. Many small chub were captured there with a red palmer. They always lay close under the opposite bank, and the fly had to fall within an inch of the clay or weeds. Sometimes a fish would rise immediately like a trout, but more often it would follow the fly for some distance, making quite a decent wave. Then the tightening line would announce the time to strike, and the half-pounder would be hooked and played. Very fair sport he would give, too, for I used to fish with a tiny greenheart rod, about eight feet six inches long, whose weight must have satisfied the most zealous light-rod man. It was the right rod for a boy, and it was also the right rod for getting the greatest amount of fun out of small chub.

Three large chub are prominent in early memories. The capture of one is described in early memories. One of them was a Wye fish, for whose better undoing I had to ascend a tree. Seated in the fork, which overhung a deep, still pool, I perceived my friend and others of lesser calibre basking on the surface. A lump of cheese paste was carefully lowered, allowed to hang in the water just before his nose, and taken. The rest is confusion, and I have no clear memory of what happened, except that it was all very exciting, and that the tree, and my rod, and the chub, and I, got much mixed up. But the fish came out at last, and weighed - I know not what. I used to call him three pounds. The other monster came later than either of the two mentioned, from the Teme, and I remember it chiefly as being the reward of patience. I fished for it persistently for two days, and at last got it on an alder.

It weighed three and a half pounds on the scales, and was a great triumph.

Chub played, on the whole, the most important part in my early fishing, and they were my earliest instructors in fly-fishing. The Thames was the scene of the first exploits, two joints of a relative's salmon rod the first fly-rod, and a one-ounce chub the first fish caught with fly. I visited the same reach again not long ago, and the glory of it is departed. Even the one-ounce chub is no longer to be caught - by me, at any rate - and the whole scene is woefully altered. It does not do to 'revisit Yarrow'. Still, one has one's memories, and I shall always think with awe of the three great perch below

the footbridge that came up out of the depths after my worm, looked at me, and went down again. On the strength of those perch I laid out three-halfpence in Abingdon on the purchase of a 'hook to gimp' - silver gimp, I remember, and very pleasing to the eye. The investment was not remunerative. That same week, however, I received a gift which was. By the backwater I came upon a grown-up angler who had a roach nearly as big as himself. He told me that it was two and a half pounds, and that he had caught it with red lead.

He gave me of this miraculous bait, and that same evening I caught a roach of three quarters of a pound, myself on a piece of it, thereby breaking my record utterly. I have never tried the bait since, but no doubt it makes a good colouring matter for paste.

It must have been about three years later when I made my first decent bag of perch, an occasion never to be forgotten. It was on Shakespeare's Avon, a mile or two above Stratford. The August day was what an August day should be, and a blazing sun had driven me into the shade of some willows which lined the stream. The basket was empty, which was not surprising, the water being clear as glass and the heat intense; even the little fish of seven or eight inches, which at that time satisfied my modest aspirations, had declined to nibble at the proffered worm.

It was, perhaps, the tempting coolness of the deep water under the trees which made me peer round one of them and look down into the stream; it was certainly a lucky accident which made me aware of vague forms moving in and out, to and fro, below the tangle of roots and red fibres. I gazed fascinated for a time, and at last, as eyes grew accustomed to the play of light through the branches above, made out the identity of the forms; they were perch, and such a shoal of them as I had never seen before. This ascertained, of course, the question arose how they were to be caught. The branches and twigs came down so low, and the trees were so close together, that plying the rod was impossible. After much deliberation I cut a withy shoot about four feet long, and tied the gut cast to it after taking off the float. Then I had an apparatus which was manageable, and with which I could get the thrilling joy of seeing the perch actually take the worm as it sank down among them, or, more often, as it was being drawn up. I do not now remember how many I caught or what they weighed, but my small creel was quite full by the time I had finished, and I think some of the captives must have been over a pound. I learnt more about perch and their ways on that single afternoon than I should have from years of orthodox float fishing. Even now the lesson that perch like a bait which moves slowly up and down still serves me in good stead sometimes. But I fear I shall never again know quite so fine a rapture as came to me at its first learning.

At about the same period I first made acquaintance with the old Priory Pond, a marvellous piece of water in an otherwise fishless part of Gloucestershire; the most desirable spot on earth, it seemed to me, when I had discovered its secrets. It was rectangular in shape, about half an acre in size, and the monks made it; so, at least, local history averred. A kind of ancient culvert connected the pond with a short creek which joined the brook, and twice every day the water ebbed and flowed under the little bridge which spanned the neck between pool and creek. Why there should be an inland tide of this sort was always something of a mystery in those days. Subsequent meditation has suggested that when the mill situate in the ancient Priory buildings started of a morning then did the water flow; when the mill stopped at the dinner-hour, then did the water ebb. The movement of the waters was repeated when the mill started again in the afternoon and when it stopped in the evening. If the monks devised this scheme of letting fresh water into the pond without turning the brook through it, they accomplished a very pretty piece of water engineering, and calculated levels with good skill in the mathematics. The arrangement was doubtless helped by the fact that another mill dammed the brook a hundred yards below, and was worked but seldom. Indeed, the streamlet scarce afforded power for two mills within three hundred yards of one another.

Besides making the pond, the monks, it is to be presumed, put in the carp also, in spite of the old legend which makes the bronze fish but a late-comer to these shores. And, having put those carp in, they could not catch them; or, possibly, they did catch one, and so filled the others with caution. Certain it was that never had a carp been taken since, at any rate by fair angling. There are, it is said, carp that will bite at honey paste, at little new potatoes, at green peas, and even at garden worms. But those of the Priory Pond would not bite at anything. The fish were extremely fat - almost round - and they rolled about beneath my very feet, much, of course, to my excitement, since I had never dreamed of monsters in such profusion, much less seen them. It happened that I had lately read instructions for carpcatching - in *The Boy's Own Paper*, I think - so I set about the venture methodically. But there were no results. Whole gardens of vegetables, pots of honey, loaves of bread were squandered, nests of wasps, hills

of ants, heaps of mixen were ransacked to make them bite, but they rolled on undismayed, uninterested. The wonder was how fish that never ate anything could be so round, so obviously bloated with excess of good living. Probably they did eat, but only after the angler was gone. The monks had taught them, in their days of comparative youth, that it was unwise to feed when a long straight thing cast its shadow over the water. And a lesson once learnt is with a carp never forgotten. What the monsters weighed none may know, but some of them were as big as market-going porkers.

When the time wasted on these insensate wretches had run into a term of weeks the roach were discovered. Little ones, indeed, had been caught now and then on the carp tackle, but no serious roach-fishing had been attempted, because the carp had been too big and too obvious. Then one day, at the time of the ebb, a little red worm was dropped casually over the bridge that crossed the culvert into the creek. The float was fixed about three feet from the hook, and swam merrily down towards the brook. But not far, for almost at once it went under as though the hook had caught on the bottom. The rod was lifted to free it, and then a gleam in the water revealed the true cause, and a gallant roach of fully one and a quarter pounds was fighting for his liberty. He was landed, the hook was re-baited, and immediately a second glittering fish with ruddy fins took his place in the battle. Before the water had ceased to ebb, a dozen handsome roach lay on the grass - a noble sight. They averaged about three quarters of a pound, and the first was the biggest. Afterwards a day was set aside for a real onslaught on the roach, and it was a day to remember. The fish bit with the enthusiasm of inexperience; probably they had never seen a hook and line before, and on the ebb they were caught literally as fast as the line could be rebaited and dropped in. On the flow they bit, too, but more gingerly, while at slack water they would only bite now and then. The catch at the close of day was far and away the biggest I ever made as a boy, and I have only equalled it once or twice since.

There was no great roach day after that. It may have been that all the big ones in the creek were caught. In the pond itself nothing over half a pound came to the net. But fishing there incidentally revealed something else that was worthy of note.

One evening a small roach that had just been hooked was seized by an invisible monster, which ran out the line and broke it. On the morrow pike tackle was brought to bear on the situation, valuable assistance being rendered by a family retainer who was as keen a fisher as I, and more expert. A small live roach was sent out with a float to entice the fish of prey. Very soon there was a run, the float went under, and stayed under. But a strike only lost the bait and hooked nothing. A second time this happened, and a third. Then the snap tackle was taken off, a strong single hook was substituted for it, and time was given at the next attack.

These tactics were in a measure successful, but only in a measure. A very powerful fish was hooked, but it went straight into some unseen obstacle at the bottom and broke the stout gut like cotton. And similar misfortunes came afterwards until the thing began to look almost uncanny; no pike could have behaved in so arbitrary and consistent a fashion.

Could those mysterious carp have anything to do with it? But at last an explanation came, as a great writhing eel was dragged up from the bottom by sheer force. It weighed three and a half pounds, but it was a mere infant compared with some of the others that had refused to come to the net. Other eels of about the same size were landed on other days, but the monsters always got away.

Among these distant waters there are only one or two trout streams proper, and they do not provide me with many memories of success. My first efforts with the fly for trout convinced me that the method was quite useless, and that such agile fish could not be hooked with bits of feather. But the year after I caught the one-ounce chublings, I rose a trout - at any rate the gardener, the first authority in my eyes, said I had done so, and I was very willing to believe him. I fancy it was rather a tame fish, for it lived in a brook running through a garden at Cirencester, and it was never alarmed at me or my ingenuous hurling of the March Brown. I do not remember any other trout in that brook, but there were some enormous minnows.

It was a year or so later when I made my first basket of trout in a little brook running into the Wye near Rhayader. The event followed close on the heels of the capture of the chub from the tree, already recorded, and was even more satisfactory. My elders and betters had regarded the chub without enthusiasm which had vexed me; as they angled themselves assiduously, I put their attitude down to jealousy. On the great day they went off to fish some private water on the Wye, and I in my wanderings came upon this little nameless stream. From it, with a worm, I extracted half a dozen trout of a quarter of a pound each, and returned triumphant, to find the older anglers talking gloomily of low water and hopeless conditions. In a word, they had two small trout between them, and I had 'wiped their eye'. They admitted it generously, and from that day I was a confirmed trout-fisher, with views on the uncertainty of the sport, and an experience whence illustrations might be drawn - with economy. But on the subject of catching trout with a fly I was, and remained for some time after, reticent. It had been pointed out to me rather forcibly that samlets were not trout, and that if one treated them as such one would go to prison. I rather feared that I had treated some samlets as trout, even going so far as to assert that they were trout; at any rate, they were all the trout that I had so far caught with the fly.

Of other trout fishing in the golden days, memories centre for the most part round a certain insignificant brook in the western Midlands, in which, year by year, I used to perform prodigies of patience, in obedience to the law that causes the angler to strive after the unattainable. Looking back, I can see that March was rather early for trout fishing in such a stream, but a schoolboy's logic rose superior to counsels of perfection. If the holidays began in March, contemporaneously more or less with the end of all coarse fishing, it followed without further argument that trout fishing began at precisely that date; holidays without fishing, of course, were an impossibility. However, there were circumstances that took away much of the reproach of anticipating the season proper.

Chief among these was the fact that the brook only contained five trout, in the portion, at least, which it was my privilege to fish. I arrived at this exactitude of knowledge by a process of reasoning based on experience, and by the thoughtful habit that grows upon one when one is accustomed to walk several miles in the evening with an empty creel swinging airily at one's back. One of these five trout I was lucky enough to catch the first March that ever I visited the place, and when I had made no more than six, or it might be seven, expeditions. He took a worm which had been left to fish by itself, while, boylike, I sought distraction and bird's nests, and he weighed six ounces - a very fine example of Salmo fario as it seemed to me, and rendered even more estimable by the trouble it was to get him out. He had taken advantage of my absence to entangle himself and the line in the roots of a willow, and it was necessary to wade in and dig him therefrom.

Over the next two seasons I will draw a veil. They yielded no trout at all, and went a long way towards instilling scepticism, pessimism, and other 'isms' that are not taught in schools into the youthful mind, and there is no need to linger over them. But the fourth season I secured a fish in a way that I am sure would have won me an 'excellent good' from old Izaak himself, upon whose instructions my actions were, in fact, based. Just below the mill pond there was a tiny backwater, not above four feet wide in most parts, and it was fringed with a wall of bushes. Here and there lay little round pools, and in one of these I discovered a monstrous fish, very much bespotted, and altogether beyond the dreams of avarice. He rose and took some floating trifle while I was peeping over the bush, and that decided me. The water was too clear for a worm, but it was possible to dibble, and I at once sought diligently for a bait.

Insect life is not abundant in March, and it took me a long time to find anything that seemed large enough for so vast a trout, but at last, under a log, I captured a beetle of some size. Whether a beetle would be any good for trout was unknown, but it was worth trying. Presently the tip of the rod was projecting over the bush, and the insect dangled over the water, descending by slow degrees to the desired spot. I dared not look over to see what happened, and had to trust to Providence to direct matters aright. Providence was kind and there was a sudden plunge, a jerk of the rod-top, and I was holding on like grim death to a trout that fought as never trout fought before - at least, in my experience up till then. Tackle, however, in the days of youth was not refined away to invisibility; the gut stood the strain easily enough, and, after quite a short time, I was rejoicing over the captive form of my opponent. He only weighed a pound when all is said, but youth does not estimate its trophies altogether from the avoirdupois standard. It sufficed that he was a larger trout than any I had caught hitherto.

So passed that season in a halo of comparative glory, but it was eclipsed by the fifth and last March that was spent by the brook. In the interval I had learnt on the other and more troutful waters some of the mysteries of fly fishing proper, and when the spring holidays came round again I proudly renounced all baser lures and sought the place with a fly rod. At the top of the backwater was a little weir, or to be more accurate, a shallow slide of water from a floodgate in the mill pond, which ran for some yards along the side of a brick wall. It had always been marked down as a likely spot, but had been diligently fished with the worm in vain. This year, however, there had been a good deal of rain in February, and the brook was full, with the result that the water-slide was increased in volume and capacity. It was not easy to get at, for it was overgrown with brambles, and on the side away from the wall was an osier-bed; but, by standing in the six inches of ripple below, it was just possible to flick a fly into the rough water, and let it come down by the edge of the wall.

These tactics were at once adopted, and a large March Brown was flicked into the foam. There was an immediate check; I tightened, thinking the fly might have caught in something, and found that the something was a trout, which at once jumped out of the water, and then rushed madly all over his circumscribed abode, to my great alarm, for he seemed much bigger than the one of the year before, and it was almost certain that he would get off or break me. Yet, in spite of forebodings, all went well; he did not attempt to run down towards me; his exertions merely exhausted him to no purpose, and in the fullness of time I got him safely into the net - a really nice fish of one and a half pounds. This was a triumph indeed, and I was tempted to stop fishing, and carry the fish joyfully home, exhibiting him to all whom I might meet on the way. But calmer counsels prevailed, and after putting him carefully in my basket on a bed of grass, I tried the runnel again, not in the hope of another fish, but from an impulse to do something. Then an astonishing thing happened. A second trout took the fly in exactly the same manner as the first, and, after not quite so long a fight, was also landed - a fish of one and a quarter pounds. Almost incredulous, I tried once more, and hooked a third fish, of about a pound, which got off. After that there were no more rises. But my cup was full to overflowing, for this one day had yielded more fish than all the years that preceded it.

This success persuaded me that I had underrated the possibilities of the brook, and induced me to fish it with great vigour. But I never saw a trout in it again. The fish I hooked and lost came to an untimely end, falling to the gun of the miller's man, to whom I foolishly and expansively revealed his whereabouts, and I believe it to have been the last of its tribe.

CHAPTER TWO

A Hope for the New Year

I have grown to be on bad terms with my fishing diary of late and it reproaches me mutely as I sit meditating at the close of the Old Year. 'Where,' it says, 'is the record of that day you spent spinning the shallows round about Ivychurch? Where the chronicle of Flood Corner and the afternoon you passed offering worms to the fish which had taken refuge there from the rich, rolling torrent outside? Where the true history of your expedition to Bishop's Meads, of the great load of ground bait the two long rods the fourteen feet of water and all the rest of it? Where is ...?' but the querulous voice of my fishing diary is not very melodious and I have quoted enough to show the nature of its complaint.

Let me admit frankly that it is a true bill. These and other episodes in my recent angling career find no place in the diary's pages and I have no intention of giving them a place for the simple reason that inscribing them would in a measure be an act of gratitude to Providence and I feel no gratitude. Providence has led me forth to the river's bank time after time, has made me carry burdens, endure labour, suffer cold, splash about in swamps and generally do what is expected of the winter angler and in return she has given me - what? One miserable pikelet, which came out attached to a spoon bait looking like a sardine attached to the edge of a dinner plate and one movement of a float which suggested something like a bite. And that is absolutely all. Never to the edge of a dinner plate and one movement of a float which suggested something like a bite. And that is absolutely all. Never in all the experience of many seasons, have I known a fishing year draw to its close so unworthily, or the fish display such a complete indifference to lures of all descriptions. Doubtless there is some reason for it. Probably the cold, wet summer delayed 'and the dry autumn prolonged' the growth of the weeds and the river bed has in consequence been fouler than is usual at this time of the year. I know that I am not the only angler in these parts who has worn a melancholy face of late, so it is not a case of individual incapacity or ill luck. But that reflection does not make me more disposed to pay Providence the compliment of writing miserable nothings in my diary. Its pages shall be as blank as the days which have been my portion.

Fishing, however, teaches nothing if it does not teach a measure of philosophy and I can recognise that at this moment on the threshold of the bright New Year there is perhaps some advantage to be snatched out of defeat, some benefit to that inner man which is part soul, part mind.

In old days I can remember approaching the New Year with anticipations and hopes of varied character but of very similar magnitude. A forty pound salmon and a five pound trout are different in kind but about equal in importance and of course I used to picture the New Year as bringing me one of each, with a modestly reserved hope that when they came to the test of weighing they might prove to be even more important. Then there were occasional big dishes of mountain trout, a succession of three-brace chalk-stream days, a few fine baskets of perch, and other fish from time to time - a really worthy brace of pike and other satisfactory things waiting for me in every succeeding cycle of the months. For was I not destined at last to find the river 'strong without rage, without o'erflowing, full,' whenever I wanted to fish in it? Might I not expect to find spring, summer and autumn in their proper places and behaving in the proper manner? Was not even winter going to prove a time of delight not over-wet nor over-cold but brisk, health-giving and apt for sport whether with grayling, pike or coarse fish? What times we used to have - in front of us! Really it makes one want to 'see in' some of the old New Years over again and to recapture a few of those old visions of what was to come.

For I cannot say that I have any grandiose expectations in regard to the year 1921. If anything else deterred me the expense of immortalising a regiment of monstrous fishes behind bent glass would be enough to check undue greed. I do not know quite what has been the increase in cost for such work, but it is no doubt at least on a par with other increases and therefore, a number of 'specimens' would positively serve as milestones along the workhouse road rather than steps to the temple of fame. Candidly, I would rather not have my 50lb pike and 70lb salmon till the general economic position is a little easier. And as for other prospects less glittering but still splendid, such as came to me of old, recent adversity has pretty well cured me of them. You cannot go out five, six or is it seven? - times and return empty-handed without recognising Hope for the jade she often is with her flattering but very doubtful tales.

Still, as I have said, philosophy comes to us all in course of time and I do not approach the New Year in any spirit of pessimism. My desires are a good deal less ambitious than they used to be. I think they might quite fairly be described as modest. In fact, I am pretty confident that even Providence will not consider me exacting. Indeed I am almost certain that the year 1921 will bring me what I want. It may be long delayed but it cannot be wholly denied. In the coming year it is surely ordained that I shall catch another fish. And so far forward into the future with all courage and good cheer!

CHAPTER THREE

A Bite and a Half

My modest petition at the beginning of this year of grace was that I might in the course of it be permitted once more to catch a fish. I now desire to render thanks to the Fates for my petition has been granted. I have caught one; and the manner of the catching seems to me worthy of record, for no stranger experience has come to me in the course of forty years of assiduous angling.

My ambition was to catch many fish. The floods had gone down, the Thames had fallen to a successful day with roach or perch if I took the necessary pains to ensure it, if that is to say, I prepared ground bait, used it with discretion and fished with reasonable patience. It was a lovely April morning in character, although by the calendar it was only Jan 28 and the sun made me mix up the scraps of bread, bran and barley meal with enthusiasm. Two rods, a folding seat, landing net, lunch, tackle and ground bait make up quite a heavy load but the sun continued to shine and I trudged away to the riverside with a light heart.

Local wisdom had recommended to me a certain bay where a backwater joined the main stream and by its side I established myself. It was a pleasant place to fish, about five feet deep with a big slow eddy in which the float could make circular tours without much trouble to its user. For winter roach fishing I like such an eddy better than a swim in the main stream. Well, I cast in ground bait and set to work. One rod was propped on the rushes and tempted perch with a bright dew worm well on the bottom. The other in my hand, followed the movements of the roach float as it travelled round, scarcely impeded by the line, which was very thin and had been greased. Nothing happened. Neither float gave a sign of life. I cast in more ground bait and carried on. Still nothing happened. I went on exercising the reasonable patience postulated earlier, and cast in yet more ground bait. Hours passed. Lunch time came and went. And still nothing had happened. And at last I grew tired of it, apostrophised local wisdom for a fraud, gathered together my belongings and turned my back on the unfriendly spot. I would now try some place which local wisdom had not recommended.

I found it in a rather turbulent pool at the top of a very small backwater – little more than a ditch – which leaves the river almost at the weirhead. I had never seen anyone fishing there, but it looked a likely place after floods, and in due course I was established as before and fishing in much the same way, except that the eddy was quicker and smaller and needed more management. Again I summoned reasonable patience to my aid and again for a long time there was no result. But at last I became aware of half a bite. The float obviously dipped. I was too astonished to do anything; but having rebaited, I prepared myself for action next time. And sure enough as soon as the same spot was reached I had a whole bite, the rod went up and I was playing something which kept low and felt heavy. I got it up at length, drew it over the net and lifted it up the bank - a splendid roach which looked to be well over one and a half pounds. Out came my little spring balance and behold I had underestimated handsomely. The fish weighed 2 lb 5oz and I was a glad angler for it was four ounces heavier than any I have ever caught before. Of course I fished with redoubled zeal after this and did not get another bite.

So my strangest day's roach fishing came to its end - one and a half bites and one roach of two and a quarter pounds (its weight at the inn afterwards) which, they tell me, is the biggest from that part of the Thames for many years. Luck does indeed play a part in fishing!

CHAPTER FOUR

On a Storm-Swept Pike Pool

An esteemed friend and brother angler once told me, with every sign of sorrow in his countenance, that there was another angler whom he loved well, but with whom he could not go fishing any more. And the reason of it was the weather which unrelentingly pursued that other angler about the kingdom. Everlasting snow marked the unfortunate man's footsteps, a mist of perpetual rain obscured his form, unceasing north-east gales beat his face, and frequent thunder rolled over his head. Moreover, my friend had discovered, these ills descended upon the unjust and the just impartially, so that whoso accompanied the victim of misfortune became a victim himself of the like. In time, it was to be feared, providence might forget to which of the two the evil weather really belonged, and might atone for forgetfulness by zealously bestowing it upon them both, so that there could be no mistake. Therefore my friend was determined to withdraw from that company while there still remained to himself some small possibility of securing the ordinary man's portion of decent fishing days - a sorry pittance, it is true, but better a good deal than the portion he sought to avoid.

To me, with memory and conscience both awake, this seems a solemn thought, and pondering over my records, I begin to wonder whether I too may not become an object of suspicion in the eyes of the brotherhood. Nearly every winter, at any rate, to wonder whether I too may not become an object of suspicion in the eyes of the brotherhood. Nearly every winter, at any rate, whenever I have been fishing I have had wretched weather, and in more than one instance a friend persuaded out by me has suffered for it. The occasion, however, of which I write found me alone. The angler who was to have been my companion prophesied evil from afar, talked about rheumatism, and stayed wisely at home. But I had heard of a big pike, and was reckless; nor did I appreciate my friend's point of view, until the first morning of fishing, when we reached the water-side soon after ten, and C., the keeper, informed me, in a matter-of-fact tone, that he was wet through already. Half an hour later I was able to return the compliment, and half an hour after that we gave it up and fled. It will take me a long time to forget the cold of that north-easter and the furious rain and the discomfort of the wet punt on the shelterless pool.

It is a curious piece of water formed in the valley of, and a few hundred yards away from, a famous trout stream by old-time excavation in quest of peat. Shallow, fringed with tall reeds (in summer, I believe, almost overgrown with them), and connected with the river by a drain at each end, it used in days gone by to form a rare stock-pond for keeping the trout stream well supplied with pike. But now strong gratings restrain esox within his own borders, and fario has many enemies the less, while the pike-fisher has an interesting preserve sacred himself. It is none the less interesting because its shallowness and clearness make it by no means easy. Long casting, patience, and quiet are essential to success, and even with all these, fish are uncertain, and there are many days on which a single run seems to be all that one can expect. During that soaking hour on the first day one fish came to the boat, a pretty, olive-backed pike of about seven pounds. After that there was a damp two mile walk to the station, and a short railway journey to headquarters and dry raiment.

The morrow opened with equal ferocity, and I had grave doubts about fishing at all. Zeal, however, triumphed over caution and an incipient cold, and I started at last by a later train. It was the thought of the big one that sustained me. He was a known fish, and had been hooked and lost by an angler a year or more before. Before starting, I requisitioned a large cork and two smaller ones. The green and white pike float and gaudy pilots had the day before seemed altogether too conspicuous in water only about three feet deep and as clear as glass. The corks being old and dirty were a great improvement. It was some time after 11 a.m. when the first cast was made from the bank. The bait had hardly been in the water for three minutes when the big cork disappeared with a pop which was audible even at that distance of thirty yards or more. I struck in haste, and since repent at leisure. The fish immediately came straight in towards the bank so quietly that I thought him only a small one. An exclamation from the keeper first undeceived me, and then I got sight of him for myself, and gasped. It was obviously the big one and no other. Having come tamely in almost to our feet, he turned with a great swirl and dashed off for the middle, making the reel scream. There was an instant when the line was not so tight as it ought to have been, and then the bait came home alone. It was very sad, but it was my own fault. I struck too soon, and gave a fraction of slack line as well, so he was almost bound to get off.

After this great misfortune the day seemed destined to be a blank and we whiled away the time by abusing the rain and discussing the monster's probable weight. The keeper, who has gaffed many a big fish in his time, estimated him at twenty-five pounds at the least. I should not be surprised to learn that he was thirty pounds, for he was a great length. I tried spinning by way of a change after lunch, but moved nothing, and lost two traces on some immovable object at the bottom. About half-past three we took to the boat for a last half-hour, in case the big one should be inclined to come again. The rain was coming down in earnest, and I had just about given up all hope when suddenly the cork went under and the reel screamed. There was no doubt about the fish being well hooked this time, and after a few brisk runs the keeper got the gaff smartly into a handsome fish of thirteen pounds. This was consoling, and I was now satisfied with my sport. It is always a joy to retrieve one's blank when it seems hopeless. And there was more to come. I cast out again considerably to the right of where the fish had taken, and almost at once had another run. When the line tightened on him the fish came quietly towards the boat for some yards, and then let go. 'Leave it there', said C., as I was about to wind in and inspect the damage. His advice was sound, and almost as he spoke the float went under again and the fish moved off at great pace. The strike went home this time, and after a not very spirited fight I got a great fish up to the gaff, and C. had it in the boat in a moment. My spring balance, which is old and rusty and inaccurate, made him eighteen and a half pounds; but on the station weighing-machine the next day he just failed to touch nineteen pounds, so, making allowance for loss of weight, I can fairly call him nineteen pounds. After this I had time for one more cast before hurrying off to catch the train, and with it I got one more fish, a five-pounder, which went in again.

The third day the wind changed to the south-west, and it rained appallingly the whole morning. C. and I sheltered behind an old boat, which we turned over on its side, so as to get some cover, and watched the corks as the live bait worked about in the vicinity of the big fish. But never a run rewarded us before lunch, and the only thing that inspired hope was a gradual brightening of the sky, which ultimately culminated in a cessation of the rain about one o'clock. Then the wind shifted towards the north, and increased steadily all day, so that though we had very little more rain, it grew very cold. One little fish came to the spoon-bait about 3 p.m., and he was the only pike I saw feeding on either day. And about 4 p.m. one of some six pounds with live bait. Both were returned, and that closed the day's and the expedition's sport. As a finish to the season, it gave me no excuse for complaint. Some there are who are, or seem to be, in the confidence of big fish, and who reckon on a twenty-pounder or so every year. To me something over twelve pounds once in a way seems as good fortune as a reasonable man can desire. If I had caught the big one as well my pride would have been too great, so things were doubtless ordered not amiss, and if any other angler repairs my error he shall have my congratulations.

CHAPTER FIVE

A Day of Tribulation

It is mercifully ordained that one's keenest memories are in general of things pleasant. The angler in reminiscent mood loves to dwell on big baskets, soft western breezes, and the other outstanding features of a roseate past. The things he has suffered in the pursuit of his recreation have left but little impression behind, and in retrospect seem but little clouds on the mental horizon. This is as it should be, for if the remembrance of pains were as vivid as the remembrance of pleasures, a man would seriously begin to wonder whether it was worth while. Yet, in spite of this beneficent ordinance of fate, there must be always days in one's angling history that one still regards with horror and indignation - days which no amount of subsequent joy has availed to obliterate.

It has always seemed to me that an undue number of them falls to my share, but this may not be a real philosophical discovery, for I have heard other men complain, apparently with some reason; they represent the limited number of occasions on which I have sworn a solemn oath to give up fishing for ever. In addition to their own inherent vileness they must, therefore, also bear the responsibility of several solemn oaths having been broken, though this last is not a charge that I would wish to press too seriously. It would have been a pity if an oath made in haste of an evening had seemed more than an expression of impatience at breakfast-time on the morrow. Only once do I remember really giving up fishing in consequence of a malign day, and in agreement with a vow made in the darkness of despair. The events that led up to the proceeding were these:

I was staying in the West Country for a fortnight's trout-fishing at the end of April. Several days had passed like some pleasant dream. The weather had been perfect, and the trout of the country fairly amenable, so that every evening I was able to display a half-pounder or so, besides the ordinary tale of takeable fish - they ran about five to the pound, and one of half a pound was an achievement. Therefore, lulled into a kind of false security, I was ill-prepared for the day when adversity came rushing against me on the wings of a northerly gale. I started by trudging four miles in wading-stockings and brogues, a tedious form of exercise. But the day before, while taking a Sunday stroll, I had seen a perfectly monstrous trout, four pounds if an ounce, and he had decided my movements of the Monday. However, when the four miles were covered, I found that the wind was tearing straight down the valley, and making it quite impossible to get a fly at him. He had to be approached from below, for overhanging trees almost met above his haunt, and no wet-fly line could be cut into the teeth of the wind. I therefore did not attempt to cover him, but waited until there should come a lull, and, in the meantime, began to fish downstream with three flies.

I had a great deal of skill in downstream fishing, and I was not surprised when almost at once a good trout robbed me of the second dropper. Nor was I surprised when, on searching for the damping-box, in which I had put some spare flies to soften the gut, I found that it had been left behind. Accidents of this kind will happen, so I shrugged my shoulder, took out my fly-book, and began to disentangle half a dozen Greenwell's glories, which had got themselves into hopeless

confusion. After a good deal of patient work I extricated one and put the gut into my mouth. Then the other five blew away and vanished utterly. As they represented my remaining stock of this valuable fly, I spent half an hour in looking for them. Then I shrugged my shoulders once more, fastened on the dropper, and returned to the fishing. In less than a minute my last Greenwell was gone in another fish. The fly-book was open once more, and a blue upright was taken out, while three red palmers were blown out, never to be seen again - by me, at all events. Looking for them, however, occupied a certain amount of time, and it was fully twenty minutes before I got to fishing again.

So far I had been content to let my line float out with the wind and settle on the water where it would; but now I desired to reach an eddy behind a big stone close to the opposite bank. To this end I attempted a cast across the wind, and failed utterly. A collar of three flies wrapped round one is an awkward thing to deal with, especially if, as in my case, the tail-fly is fixed in a wading-sock, the first dropper in the landing-net, and the second in the small of one's back. It took me some time to rearrange matters, to replace the second dropper, which broke when I was taking off my coat, and to hunt for the four red spinners which I had the misfortune to lose when I opened my fly-book. But at last I got to work again, and began to realize that, in spite of the gale, the fish were rising in a remarkable manner. Almost every time the flies touched the water I could feel a pluck, but never a fish hooked himself or allowed me to hook him, until at last a big fellow took the tail-fly with a plunge.

There may be men who, during a gale, can control a three-quarter-pound trout at the end of a long line down-stream in rough water on gossamer gut, but I am not one of them, and very soon I was searching for the six hare's ears that had been blown out of my book while I was selecting a new tail-fly. I did not find them, and there is no need for me to describe the search. It resembled the searches that had preceded it and those that came after. Never in my life have I lost so many flies in one morning, and I believe that I have never risen and lost a greater number of fish. They seemed madly on the feed, and had it been only possible to fish upstream, I am certain I should have made a big basket. As it was I pricked trout, played them, lost them, lost flies in them, and did everything but land them. Finally I left a whole cast in a bush over deep water, and retired from the unequal contest. I judged it well to give myself time to get calm, if that were possible, so I withdrew to the foot of the moorland hill, sat down with my back to the river, and endeavoured to think of Job. It seemed to me that I could have comforted him a little by contrasting his case with mine, though I did not see where any comfort was to come from for me. But by meditating on one's wrongs I suppose one gets comforted automatically, and presently I plucked up enough spirit to eat my sandwiches, and they did me good. The discovery that I had left my flask behind with the damping-box seemed but a slight thing in comparison with the tremendous evils of the morning, and I drank a draught of pure water from a rill trickling through the moss resignedly.

After this I began to realize that the wind had dropped a little, and at once thought of my four-pounder. If only he could be caught the rest did not matter. A new cast was selected and soaked in the rill, and to it I attached a good big March Brown. Then I returned to the river, and made my way upstream to the monster's haunt. He lay at the head of a long still pool, and from watching him the day before I had gathered that he moved up into the ripple to feed, and that he had a certain beat. I intended, therefore, to fish carefully up this beat, trusting to find him somewhere along it. The wind was now considerably abated, and by wading along one side under the bushes, and casting across and upstream, it was possible to cover the necessary expanse of water. This I proceeded to do, and as this is a tale of woe there is no need to dwell on details. The fish, or a fish of great size, at any rate, was just where I expected, took the fly with a rush, ran out twenty yards of line, leaped twice, ejected the fly, and was gone in about half a minute, leaving me to my thoughts of Job and his exaggerated griefs.

After this I wandered upstream for a long way without troubling to fish until the crowning misfortune of the day fell upon me. For some distance the river had run through open moorland, but now I came to a field and surmounted a stile. Halfway across I became aware of approaching thunder, and looking round, perceived that a herd of cattle was stampeding in my direction, apparently of set purpose.

To avoid unprofitable argument, I stepped hurriedly down the steep bank into the river, which was just not deep enough to over-top my waders. The cattle reached the bank above, and watched me with indignation as I began to make my way across. Then, as though by concerted arrangement, a fresh enemy appeared on the other side - a big, evil-looking black dog, which had the air of one accustomed to protect homesteads. It stood and waited for me in grim silence. Then it was that I took the solemn oath to give up fishing, not only for that day, but for all time, if only I should win safely out of my parlous situation. I have no doubt that there was nothing to fear from either dog or cattle, but my nerves were upset by calamity. The rest is a tale of splashing downstream until I got back to the moor below the cattle and away from the dog. Incidentally I broke the top of my rod and filled my waders, and had to walk home in dire discomfort and in heavy rain. As to the solemn oath, it was kept for a whole day. The day after, however, was the perfection of fishing weather, and the river had fined down nicely.

CHAPTER SIX

In a Welsh Valley

To the convinced trout fisher it is not essential to have a constant succession of red letter days or to keep up a two pound average. No one esteems either benefit more than I, but I can manage to get along quite happily without them and so can the rest of the little company which assembles year by year on the bank of the small Welsh river, which I always call the Penydwddwr. It is now some years since we were all together there - war has upset many a good old custom - but odd members of the party have been there at some time or other since 1914 and now that it is possible to look forward again, great plans are being laid for a united descent upon the well-loved valley.

The Penydwddwr is a typical Welsh trout stream, that is to say a typical upland trout stream. So far as I have visited them I have found very little difference between the mountain streams of any part of the kingdom. Even the variation in the size of the trout which is noticeable is, I think, more a matter of a stream's normal development than any special characteristics.

The further a river runs from its rocky beginnings, the richer the land through which it winds and, in consequence, the more bounteous its food supplies and the fatter its trout.

Some of the famous mountain streams, such as the Usk or the Don, have a greater proportion of rich land to their mileage than others which produce smaller trout.

But even some of the barrenest rivers may have their fertile reaches. Nothing, I should say, could well be more suggestive of an eight-to-the-pound average than the top part of the Cumberland Derwent. In a solid week's fishing round about Seathwaite I think I only got one trout which exceeded six ounces. That was some twenty years ago, but I do not suppose that conditions have altered since then. Lower down, however, it is a very different story. One day below Cockermouth a few years back I got a dozen trout which averaged half a pound and I heard of a catch of a dozen or more which averaged over one pound. The lower Derwent is naturally rich in fly and on the day recorded I saw the biggest hatch of Iron Blues that has ever gladdened my eyes. Of course I had no such thing as an iron blue in my fly book and I had to make shift with the darkest hackle fly I could find. It served fairly well, but if I had some real Iron Blues I might have caught some bigger fish and more of them. I never saw trout rise with more enthusiasm for an hour or so.

I have not had enough opportunities to be didactic about it, but I fancy that wet fly streams and parts of them, could be divided into about three classes so far as the size of fish is concerned: (a) The very barren, rocky streams and parts where seven or eight fish would be needed to weigh a pound and where the exceptional half-pounders have big heads and long lean bodies. (b) The normal streams and parts where a five-to-the-pound average is to be expected. Here the half-pounder is better shaped and looks less of a cannibal. (c) The rich streams and parts where the average goes up to three-to-the-pound and where you may expect a sprinkling of pounders and may hope for an occasional fish of two pounds or even more.

The Penydwddwr, where I know it, belongs to the normal class and it is not so lavish of its half-pounders as to make us blasé in regard to them. We have, in fact, in that valley a very proper respect for a half-pounder. Indeed, the word 'respect' is scarcely adequate. You really ought to hear Caradoc tell the story which takes him cast by cast to the very top of the run below the bluff and which ends with two leaps, one despair and the words 'a real big fish, my dear fellow, half a pound.' Having heard this, you will understand how it is with us, with Caradoc, with the school master, with the ornithologist, with the angler to whom I must make only the most distant reference and with me. And those others, the estimable folk who inhabit the same inn with us, also appreciate a half-pounder. They know how long and broad and deep and thick he feels when you lay an eager hand on him in the meshes of the landing net. Persons who only fish in chalk-streams have no inkling of the merits of half-pounders. 'Just not sizeable' is a poor way in which to speak of fishes which make Caradoc arise early in the morning, pedagogues forget the Greek for 'strike,' bird men accept a statement that a cuckoo in winter turns into a hawk. All which strange things I have, so to speak, watched happening.

One spring we had a drought and then it was lamentable but true that half-pounders did not happen at all, not the real, unquestionable, eight-ounce-to-the-half-pound creatures which alone pass the severe inspection of Ap Evan. I did all that I could in the way of asseveration for a seven ounce specimen brought back one evening by the rod fourth on my list. If that were not a half-pounder, then might I never behold half-pounders more - and so on.

But it was all no use. Seven ounces were all that Ap Evan and the scales would concede when it came to the ultimate test.

We had, for sheer self-respect, to fall back on the classification method, invented I believe by the bird man in one of his inspired moments. By that device you really can catch some half-pounders in the Penydwddwr and it is an ill day on which you do not have at least one. It is quite a scientific plan of grouping your fish into growth classes rather than labelling each one with pedantic minuteness. You find something like it in Blue Books. By this method 'half-pounder' is a group term inclusive of all grades of fish from six and a quarter ounces to eight ounces. The next group contains 'big fish,' which may vary from four and three-quarter ounces to six and a quarter ounces. Then come the quarter-pounders, inclusive, of course, of 'rising' quarter- pounders. Decent fish follow, separated by some little margin from 'breakfast' fish. And lastly the bird man rose superior to the droughts and dearth of that hard time with 'visible' fish. It was a handy new group and generally approved.

The river was lower than it possibly could be when we got there and it went on dwindling for a solid week. Daily we went out with less hope of doing anything and daily we came in justified of our expectations. Even 'visible' fish were loth to rise, while all others became events. 'Did you do anything on the long flat?' one would ask. To which another would reply, 'Yes, I had quite a brisk bit of sport there. Got two breakfast fish, and lost a real big one, a quarter-pounder at least.' The 'big one which got away' was, I think, unusually prominent that year. He afflicted me personally to a grievous extent.

Perhaps the worst experience was with the detestable button on the sleeve of Caradoc's mackintosh. It was on the last day of all, when we really had had a nice drop of rain and the river was in grand order. In quite a short time during the morning I had accumulated five handsome fish, of which two were half-pounders by the class test. But then trouble began, for the wind uprose and beat the rain on my glasses, no fish stirred, I lost half a cast and both the flies and generally things went wrong. Just as I was getting desperate I hooked a fine trout and my spirits went up with a bound. He played fast and far, but I was his master. That trout, half-pounder though he might be, was as good as in the basket. I felt with unhurried left hand for the net in the sling, meanwhile drawing the trout downstream. And then the button on the sleeve saw fit to catch in the meshes of the net and in a flash my mastery was gone. Not only could I not get the net out; I could not even free my left hand. So in due course the trout kicked himself off, leaving me alone with the wind and the rain and the conviction that all was over. I do not wish to blame Caradoc in any way - after all, he had kindly lent me the garment and that it failed to keep the rain out was not his fault - but I do blame the button. Anglers ought to tie themselves together with tapes or string, not imperil their immortal souls by the use of buttons.

The chub also lost me a fine trout the day before by swinging about my legs and nearly upsetting me at the critical moment. I had better explain the chub. There were nine of them, weighing from about three-quarters of a pound to a pound and a half and they were the fruits of an amusing hour or so at the pool by the wall. The custom of the river is I believe, to kill chub in the most violent manner possible and then to kick them about the landscape, cursing as you kick. Truly chub are not wanted in a small trout stream, but I have an affection for those despised fish and besides, nine of them made a brave show and might be valued by some poor body.

So, since they were too big and many for my little creel, I slung them on a leather bootlace presented to me for other purposes by the school master and slung that to the landing net sling. An uncommon nuisance they were, eleven or twelve pounds of them a-dangle and as I have said, they nearly upset me when I was playing the best trout of the day. After that I declined to be burdened with them more, dragged them to the nearest roadway and there left them, in the hope that the not impossible poor body would find them for himself. I have reason to believe that this happened, for the next day the chub were gone. It may have been that the poor body coveted the bootlace. One never knows.

The gravel bed caused us all bad quarters of an hour from time to time that spring. The gravel bed is an inferior sort of fly which appears in vast numbers and makes the trout go half mad - not quite mad - just not so mad as to take any sort of artificial fly. Ap Evan had two counsels for coping with the gravel bed rise. One was to use something else, as a March Brown or Half Stone. The other was to give the affair up as hopeless. My feeling is that he thought more highly of the second plan. Yet people do catch trout during gravel bed rises; and some describe the opportunity afforded by them as a thing not to be missed.

All I know is that we made nothing of the business. Some of us even - so it was reported - danced with rage at seeing so many and so big trout moving without being able to catch them. It was a new experience to see trout moving in numbers in the Penydwddwr. It was a new experience also to see abundance of fly, not only gravel bed, but also March browns and the spinners thereof, besides smaller kinds. And it was new also to have warm weather. If only there had been a decent quantity of water! But the water came as our time was practically up. 'Tis ever thus.

I have said that there were no genuine half-pounders. Nor were there, but one evening we were all staggered to behold a trout of some fourteen inches' length which weighed within a trifle of a whole pound. It was a portent and we stood in a dumb row before it, wondering how such a thing might be. It had been hooked in a fin, moreover, and had kept its captor in play for some ten minutes. You might go to Penydwddwr many times without seeing such another. But you might see my three-and-a-half-pounder in the big flat if you looked close. I saw him one evening and came home and talked about him at length, not unmindful of the proverb about 'having lived near the rose.' On the whole, I did well out of the incident. It was unlucky that I should see him again a day or so after. I found that while men slept he had turned into a chub. People laugh easily at Penydwddwr. I had made similar little mistakes there before. I question whether honesty is invariably the best policy. But, on the other hand, had someone else discovered the truth they would have laughed more. Perhaps honesty stands where it did.

The most remarkable incident of the expedition was the humour of the bird. It pounced down upon the artificial fly of one of the anglers. That was no uncommon thing. It had happened to me often. But I had never before heard of a fowl with such a sense of fun that, having seized the fly, it would carry it to the top of a tree and leave it there. If any should doubt, we were told that the fly was there yet and half a cast with it and that any one might prove the matter by climbing.

Another spring visit to the Penydwddwr Arms was spoilt by an exactly opposite condition of affairs, due, it was supposed, to comets, of which there had been much talk. We had many trials that year. Apart from the weather, we found that the local farmers had had a burst of energy and had been consolidating their fences. We spent a good deal of time extricating ourselves from the traps they had set and it was a warmly discussed problem why barbed wire was necessary as a lining to trout streams, in some places reinforcing stout hedges and serviceable railing and whether, as one angler gloomily opined, it had been arranged with one eye on beasts and the other on the fishermen.

The Welsh farmer is not invariably sympathetic. Nor are his bulls, of which we discovered an unusual profusion that year. They glowered at us in all sorts of unexpected places. Given plenty of barbed wire, a river in half flood and rising and a bull waiting for you to come out of it and you have your day's excitement fully provided.

The sort of weather we all had can be gauged by the fact that from time to time one of us would rise silently from his chair and step from the sitting room into the hall. Then would come the sound of hammering - the barometer. Our landlord, easygoing man that he is, even he was moved to protest. He said that the instrument could not be expected to do its honest duty when beaten like that. Whereupon Caradoc told him the story of the irate gentleman who threw his expensive but unresponsive barometer into the garden with the remark,

'Go and see for yourself, you beast!' Certainly our barometer did very strange things. It climbed to a giddy height, leaped suddenly down to 'much rain,' and then climbed again just as quickly. Perhaps there ought to be a mark for comets on barometers.

While I was away a dry fly friend wrote to ask why I was wasting time over 'Welsh minnows,' a question begotten of a recent victory over a five-pounder in the Kennet. He would have had his answer had he felt the thrill that I felt on the one satisfactory day when waist-deep in the chub pool I saw that I had hooked, not after all a chub as I feared, but a veritable trout of great size. He weighed half a pound, a real half pound and the joy that seized me when I saw him, to be followed by immediate quaking lest he might get off, was certainly no less than which was mine at mayfly time when a supposed chub proved to be a noble Kennet trout of three and a half pounds. In the evening I got another half-pounder in the same pool and the brace will live long in the memory, if only for the effectual manner in which they enabled me to answer Caradoc, who also had one and was prematurely jubilant over it.

One day, rendered desperate by the weather, I angled with worm in a flood and tore out several unfortunate trout by brute force. Time was when I thought worming in pea soup eddies the height of bliss and I was curious to see if the glamour of youth could be recaptured. There is a moment - I have before confessed it - when you live at this business, the moment in which you felt the first twitch at the line as a trout essays the worm. Nor will I deny that the four quarter-pounders which I got out of the little channel below the mill wheel gave me pleasure, nor that, as the six ounce fish fell back, I lived once more some of the old agony. These things

I confess. But there came a moment when I was conscious of blood and slime and that I was engaged on a very black venture. And, moreover, I had no half-pounder. So I put away worms and fished to no purpose with a Devon minnow. We had that day a hail storm which gave me a cold. It was incredibly fierce and chilled me to the marrow, so that I had to go home to get early tea and warmth.

On the last day of that visit I had a useful lesson in humility. The 'local expert' had always appeared to me an overrated person. In London I had ventured to state in conversation that he was not likely to be much more successful than any visitor of reasonable skill. I had to retract all that. I toiled exceedingly all that cold day, struggled with an abominable wind, fished, methought, very well considering and returned at tea time with eleven fish, convinced that all that man could do in the way of tempting sulky trout had been done by me and that my basket represented the limit of possibility. But I found that Ap Evan had been out and between about half past one and four had captured some two dozen very nice fish, all with the March Brown, a fly which had caught me nothing at all. The fact is that local experts are very fine fellows; we visitors are nought.

The biggest fish I caught at all was, oddly enough, a dace of nine ounces, a fish which, so far as I could learn, had never been caught there before, though chub are fairly plentiful. I saw it rise at the tail of a long flat and put my tail fly over it dry. The disappointment of finding that it was not a good trout was somewhat mitigated by the interest of its identity. I think it was envy which made certain persons asseverate that it was a chub, in defiance of all the indications of shape and fins. The oddest experience I had was being spectator of an affray between a sparrowhawk and two thrushes. I was knee-deep in a quiet pool when I suddenly became aware of a commotion in the hedge that bordered the water on the left bank, of great fluttering, out-cry and flying of feathers, all not five yards from me. It proved that the hawk was attacking a thrush, probably on its nest. Then the thrush's mate arrived in a hurry and some further battle ended with one bird flying away with the hawk in pursuit and the other vanishing, perhaps following on the other side of the hedge. I hope the hawk got defeated, but events passed beyond my ken.

The most vivid realisation of Penydwddwr as a place unspoilt and good to be in perhaps came when I conversed with the friendly policeman. Comets and aeroplanes were the topics and then he told me about the balloon. It passed over the district one misty day, to the unqualified terror of the inhabitants, who had never seen or heard of such a thing. Flying low, it almost grazed the hill beyond the river and a lonely shepherd caught sight of a rope hanging from the miraculous bird or whatever it might be. This, running, he vainly tried to seize and fell flat. And as he fell to his horrified amaze he heard mocking laughter from the skies. Wonder was not dead then, though even at Penydwddwr they must now be used to men who travel with the clouds.

The last visit I paid to Penydwddwr was shortly before the war and it was at an unaccustomed time of the year. The fact was that I had heard of salmon there if one was on the spot during August floods, and it struck me that a salmon or two a day from those little pools would be very pleasant amusement. So it would be if it ever happened, but so far as I could judge it does not happen.

Caradoc, who exhibited symptoms of jealousy when he heard I was going said 'I told you so,' as soon as I had returned.

For I had to confess that the expedition, from the point of view which regards heaps of slain fishes at the *summum bonum*, had not been a complete success. Not that I would impute such a point of view to Caradoc. In the spring we do not pile our fishes in heaps. We say that we do not like our fishes so, that a few trout, and those good ones, are what we prefer. And we get the few trout all right, while as to goodness I never met any that were better on a breakfast table. There are, be it noted, different kinds of goodness which trout may have. An ability to stretch head and tail beyond a dish does not exhaust the cardinal virtues.

Accustomed to the Penydwddwr of spring, I was astonished and saddened at the stream which greeted our eyes on arrival. The Colonial, who was one of my companions and who has since eschewed my company on fishing holidays, was of the opinion that it would be rather like the thing called 'a creek,' only the creeks where he came from had water in them which ran along. (I shall never get quite reconciled to the notion of Greater Britain that a creek is a small stream, a burn or beck; to me the word always suggest a convenient ditch by the Thames into which you can run your punt). Closer inspection showed us that the Penydwddwr was moving along, for 'even the weariest river winds somewhere safe to sea,' but it was patent that the fishing would be nought until what the third member of the party called the 'great rains' should come. As for the fourteen-foot and sixteen-foot rods which formed part of my armament, they were as out of place by the attenuated stream as a racing eight would have been upon it. I took them, blushing, and hid them in a corner.

Then we composed ourselves to await the great rains. There were kingfishers, herons and other birds to be seen daily on the stream. In the little wood behind the garden were three brown owls, of which we could generally obtain a view by going cautiously to look for them. Their large round eyes would look down at us reproachfully from the upper branches and their large round bodies would sooner or later remove noisily to a less visible perch. I got the impression that, nocturnal though they be, brown owls can see quite well enough in the day to serve all their necessities.

In the roadway before the inn door commonly strutted an important turkey cock. I was privileged to behold this bird in two sets of circumstances of delightful contrast. A little lady emerged from the inn one day. She wore a red tie, but had about her no other sign of fierceness or offence. Suddenly across the road came a resonant gobble and the big bird came purposefully from the farm yard, giving his opinion as he came. 'What a funny bird,' was the amused greeting he received, as he stalked majestically on. Amusement, however, gave place to hesitation, for he came closer and closer and his gobbling waxed louder and louder. And the next thing was a vision of flying skirts - the red tie and its wearer were gone and the turkey was alone in his glory.

On the other occasion from out the door came not a lady, but an eight-weeks-old black spaniel puppy. This waddling atom saw the dignified bird but two yards away. To see was to act and we had the inestimable privilege of beholding a turkey hunt conducted by a pack of one. Nothing could have been more ludicrous that the ignominious flight of so large a bird before so small and round a pursuer.

Besides birds there was a rich vegetable world to study. Development seemed to be a month later than in the south and the meadows were rich with hay and with some of the flowers which had greeted me in Hampshire in June. The lanes winding upward to the moors contained quite a store of wild strawberries, which gave us an agreeable kind of mild hunting and here and there were wild raspberries, of excellent flavour. Of an evening, too, there was occasionally an Eisteddfod to which one listened out of the window. Several really beautiful voices well maintained the reputation of Wales for folk music.

This, of course, is not fishing, but I am not sure whether our actual efforts with the rod were much better deserving of the name. We frankly pottered, limiting our ambitions to getting enough trout for breakfast and occasionally making a raid on the chub. Here I have an observation on gratitude to make. It had struck me that the Colonial was getting 'kind of homesick.' He did not consider the Penydwddwr a real creek - in real creeks you can, it appears, catch brook trout in dozens on No. 6 flies and you take them home on a string - and his baskets had been light. 'What you must do,' I said, 'is to have a go for the chub.' 'What are chub?' he asked without enthusiasm. 'Chub are...' I hesitated for a comparison, 'I know. Chub are just like squaw fish.'

His eyes brightened. The good old squaw fish - it was like a message from home, though, I have gathered from his conversation, at home the squaw fish is not exactly a prized trophy. Anyhow, I had rekindled hope in his breast and he had a go for the chub.

That evening I returned to find that he had captured a really considerable chub, a fish of nearly three pounds, which is big for the Penydwddwr. Was he pleased? He was not. He thought meanly of the chub. He spoke meanly of it. He regarded the escape of just such another not as a misfortune, but as an incident of no importance. Didn't they fight? No, not worth naming. Weren't they like squaw fish? No - gloomily - squaw fish had teeth. And he was not a bit impressed by the chub's throat teeth, as described. Altogether the matter turned out disappointingly and it was not long after when the Colonial 'hit the ties,' 'boarded the cars,' or whatever Greater Britain calls going by train and went off to London to see about some 'real estate,' or 'preemptions,' or 'town lots,' or something. Nor did he return.

Meanwhile I went on waiting for the great rains. Not a drop was granted to us, though clouds appeared promisingly on several occasions and though once we even heard the rumble of thunder in the hills. For the most part we had blazing, windless days and it was only by dry fly in shady corners or by drop-minnow in the deeps that I could extract a few trout while the light was strong. Now and then I went out and caught breakfast between dusk and dark, a dragging of big flies which involves little skill and some alarms.

The riverside at night is an unfamiliar place, full of queer shapes and uncanny noises. On the whole I did not do so badly considering. Though the trout were few and to be counted by the brace rather than by the dozen, they ran to a better size than they do in spring. Then I have found the average size on a decent day to be under four ounces. On this last visit the trout I caught averaged between five and six ounces and a fair proportion reached the half pound. Moreover, there were the chub, of which I took toll daily and with which I had plenty of fun. Chub in a low, clear mountain stream require a lot of stalking and the sport was not to be despised.

There was also one salmon which took a shrimp and a few other salmon which would not take anything. Only the first deserves more than passing notice and he, not because he was caught, but because he took at all. He was lying in less than four feet of water near the bank and I was hiding behind my own rod, as a friend puts it, when I angled for him. He must have seen the rod and me, clearly and yet he took the shrimp the moment it came near him. If only we had had rain, even a little rain, to freshen things up, I believe some of his fellows would have proved equally accommodating. But we had no rain. If I live to be a very old man and visit Penydwddwr twice or thrice a year, I have hopes of some day getting the right conditions for fishing. Then it would be something uncommonly like Paradise.

CHAPTER SEVEN

May Day on the Exe

' Six weeks every year among crag and heather,' is Charles Kingsley's prescription for the Londoner's holiday; and, all things considered, it is no bad one. If he is a comparatively free agent, he may apportion them more or less according to his pleasure. For my own part I incline to a fortnight in spring, the last week of April and the first of May, and the rest divided between August and September. This is, of course, only individual preference, and is inspired by the fact that I must have my spring trout-fishing even at the cost of suffocating in London during July.

There are many people who agree with me. About the middle of April you shall often see a contemplative person standing with his back to the busy throng and his face to a fishing tackle shop. If you are in a gloomy mood you may moralise at sight of him on the vanity of human wishes, and picture to yourself the horrid gnawing at the soul of the man, the regret for the holidays in past years never to be enjoyed again; but if, on the other hand, you are cheerful and pleased with the world, you may look on him as a pretty picture of pleasant indecision, merely perplexed as to whether he will want two dozen large March Browns or three dozen, and wondering whether the bushes are going to be as deadly to flies this year as they were last. I believe that this cheerful view is the right one to take, for if he cannot get his holiday your angler becomes morose and avoids tackle shops and all that may remind him of what he is losing.

Yes, a man who gazes at the wares in a tackle shop on a sunny day in April has certainly a fishing expedition in prospect. It would be too terrible to imagine a poor wretch with the spring and the streams calling to him unable to obey the call. There is nothing more sacred, more inviolable, than this spring fishing; it is one of the laws of Nature, and not the least important. Before the angler would consent to give it up, he would turn highwayman and rob omnibuses in the Strand to procure funds, or blow up the Houses of Parliament and disorganise the kingdom to procure leisure. He *must* fish, in fact. If the shattered globe were falling to pieces about his ears he would be found hurrying off to his favourite stream, rod in hand, that he might perish there decently and in order - always provided, of course, that the lamentable event happened about the end of April. Against all reason, too, he must have his spring fishing. Tell him that the east wind blows constantly in April and May, that if he waits till the beginning of June he will be able to catch much finer and fatter trout with the Mayfly in streams much nearer home; it is all in vain; he will shake his head, admit the force of your arguments, and say that he is going down to the West Country by the first train tomorrow.

Opinions differ as to which part of the country offers most attractions to the trout fisher in spring. Many a tempting adviser would tell us to go north. By the negative process (than which is none more insidious), Mr Andrew Lang has almost made up my mind more than once to start for Clearburn Loch, for 'there are trout in Clearburn.' Here is his additional recommendation: 'There are plenty in the loch, but you need not make the weary journey; they are not for you or me,' The weary journey shall certainly be made one day, not of course that I want to prove Mr Lang in the wrong, but because of the perversity of human nature, which insists on trying conclusions with fate, every man for himself. Moreover, there is always the chance that the trout of Clearburn may have changed their habits.

Then there is the great dry fly school, which would inspire a man to cast the May Day fly in southern Test or Itchen. There are patriotic Irishmen who have written witching words about their witching country, and whose descriptions of its trout fishing are fully justified. The principality also has its prophets; and there are good men and true who would go no farther than deep-bosomed Thames, for he holds out vague promises of monster trout to the man who seeks them with skill and patience. In short, choice is manifold. But, after all, experience is the only safe guide.

I remember spending the whole of a spring day waiting for the rise by the side of Sprinkling Tarn, the most gloomy piece of water in Cumberland, that looks as if Nature had buried some monstrous crime beneath its dark water. Rumour ran that there were trout in it, many and good, and I waited patiently till dark, but never a fish rose, and to this day I know

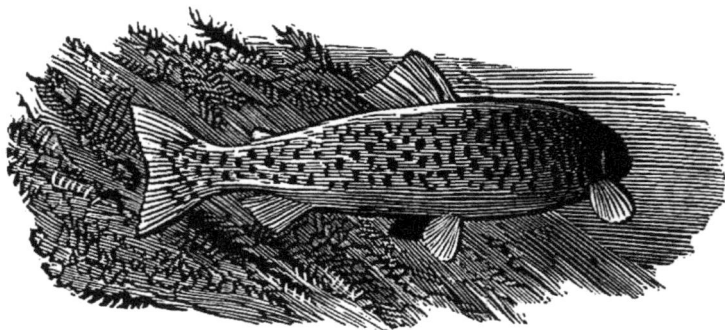

not if there are fish there. Therefore I cannot recommend it for trout, but if there be any man with an unduly good conceit of himself who is anxious to adjust his ideas, a few spring hours by Sprinkling Tarn would be just the thing for him. I know no piece of scenery so certain to make a man realise what a worm he is when taken out of his context. There are trout in the Sty Head Tarn on the pass a few hundred feet below, so after he has received his object lesson and has humbled himself he can do some fishing there if he wishes.

But, though I love it well, I would not go to Cumberland for my May Day. Rather do I hasten as fast as express train can bear me to the ancient town of Taunton, and thence by a quaint simple-minded line (the forerunner of the switchback) to the other ancient town of Dulverton, and thence by road up the valley of the Exe to the prettiest village in Somersetshire. The wise man, when he gets to Dulverton, will send his luggage, indeed, by the dogcart that is waiting for him, but himself, for it is but three o'clock in the afternoon, will walk. He may, if he pleases, breast the opposite hill and plunge straight into the moor, so shall his journey be shorter in point of miles. But the man just escaped from London should acclimatise himself to Exmoor gradually; it is a little overpowering to step straight on to it from Paddington, and moreover, if it is his first visit, he may get lost.

Therefore let him take my advice and follow the road that runs by the Exe, not hurriedly as the earnest pedestrian, but leisurely as befits the man with a whole fortnight of spring before him. It is a friendly road, amiably winding, with just enough of undulation to make him glad that he goes, as he was meant to go, on his two feet and not on two ridiculous wheels. Also there are soft mossy places for him to sit with primroses and dog violets for company, while he considers the wonderful young green which the bushes beside the road are timidly putting forth. And while he sits the yellow-hammers, and perhaps a squirrel, will come and look at him and give him friendly greeting, as do all things on Exmoor to him that comes in a right leisurely spirit. Above all, the Exe will talk to him from its bed below, and will explain that, though here near Dulverton it is a considerable river, nearly as big as its cousin Barle, and has its great weirs almost worthy of Severn, and in these weirs are the salmon, yet after he has gone a few miles up he will find it but a small stream, lively and clear as crystal, and ready to talk to him the whole of the rest of the way. Just here, however, it must leave him, because it has to go and attend to its weirs.

For about a mile the river and the road separate with the whole breadth of the valley between them. Afterwards, as the valley narrows they are never very far apart, and sometimes they are so close that the bank of the road is also the bank of the river. Here our traveller can look down and see every pebble on the bottom of the stream, so clear is the water. But look as he may he cannot see what he is chiefly anxious to see - fish. The trout of a mountain stream to the eye accustomed to pavements are practically invisible, except in the deep still pools. On a chalk stream, with a little practice and with the sun at a proper angle, you can see every movement of the fish you are stalking; but in the mountain stream you have to fish in the hope that he is there. In the deep still pools, however, it is generally possible to see two or three elderly fish swimming about near the surface on the look-out for flies.

An elderly fish in the Exe is not a giant like his cousin of the Itchen. He attains his half pound in weight and is proud of it, and the fisherman who catches him is proud too, for the Exe half pounder compels respect both by reason of his scarcity and of his fighting powers. Never shall I forget the one that bolted down-stream with me as soon as he was hooked, forcing me to splash after him for several minutes. I thought him a two pound fish at the very least, and could hardly believe my eyes when he finally came to the net. If a brace of half pounders is in one's basket at the end of a day's fishing it is a matter for congratulation, and reason enough for displaying the catch to the passer-by. And yet there are the big fish even in the Exe. There is, or was, one in a weir pool which our friend passes, a fish that would not make an inconspicuous figure in the Thames. I have had a glimpse of him myself, and I thought he must be a salmon, but was assured that he was a trout. His dimensions and weight, if I gave them, would only be guesswork; and as they might not be believed they shall not be given.

I can, however, testify to several fish in some of the big pools along the side of the road which must be well over two pounds, and that is, or ought to be, enough for the most greedy of fishermen - if he can catch them, for I believe them to be beyond the power of man's flies. I have spent many fruitless days trying for them, and have even been so unorthodox as to tempt them with a dry fly, but have never yet induced one of them to rise. A local expert once told me that he had caught a trout of four pounds in one of these pools some years ago; but somehow his methods of narrative were not convincing.

Even the small fish of the Exe are not to be caught by throwing flies at them. Upstream must you fish, and hard must you work, to basket two dozen, and the finest tackle is none too fine. It is one of my theories that they are harder to catch than the trout of the Barle over in the next valley, and that the reason of it is as follows. A great deal of the bed of the Barle is composed of rocks covered with dark water moss, and the result is that the water of the Barle is in general darker than that of the Exe, in which there is comparatively little of this moss, and so the trout are more readily taken in with artificial flies. But whenever you do come across a patch of this moss in the Exe, fish over it very carefully, and it is odds that your basket will be the better for it.

But while we have been gossiping, our light hearted-traveller has walked a good distance up the valley. He has refreshed himself with excellent ale (to the right-minded man on his holiday there is no such thing as beer) at a wayside hostelry; he has gulped in the spring in great draughts, and is fully conscious how good a thing it is to be alive and out of London. Now he is leaning over a little bridge contemplating Quarme Water. The Quarme is a lively little stream which runs into the Exe at the point where two valleys meet, for here the Exe turns a sharp corner and comes out of a valley to the left. The Quarme, too, is famous for the quality of its trout, but it is difficult to fish, being much overgrown. Both Exe and Quarme are preserved, but our fisherman has obtained leave to fish as much water as he can cover in a fortnight, for the hospitality of Exmoor will stand even the most searching of tests, the request for permission.

From this point it is but a short two miles to the prettiest village in Somerset, our friend's destination, where is the prettiest inn in the world and the warmest welcome. Here the wayfarer finds a solid tea ready for him, and he is quick to perceive, and to take advantage of the dish of cream which is one of its attractions. This cream would lead the most dyspeptic into error, but many things may be done and eaten in Exmoor air which in London would cause sorrow of heart and body.

After his tea he goes out and strolls up the village street and lays out a small sum in procuring a licence to fish, for even when you have leave from the owners of the water you must further arm yourself with a licence, which is a thing worth knowing. Ignorance of this necessity has led well-known people into error and fines. The licence obtained, his steps turn naturally and unbidden in the direction of the principal bridge (the prettiest village in Somerset has several bridges), and there he meditates with his elbows on the parapet and his pipe going sweetly to his satisfaction.

The bridge habit comes as easily to, and sits as gracefully upon, the angler as the oldest inhabitant. Indeed, unless he is at times given to meditating on bridges, I doubt if he is a true angler at all. In Somerset they know how to build bridges, with well dispositioned parapets, neither so high that one cannot lean on them in comfort and see into the pool below, nor so low that one is in danger of falling over on a dark night. One of the reasons why the angler almost always leans over a bridge, if there is one, is that the said bridge generally gives shelter to the largest trout in the neighbourhood. If he is a well known trout and respected by the inhabitants he may be seen lying a foot or so below the bridge waiting for the worms which are thrown to him from time to time by his admirers. There is a bridge over another river, the midland Lambourn, below which are half a dozen trout constantly in waiting for pellets of bread, and I have there seen as many stalwart anglers, each with his slice of bread, solemnly making votive offerings.

And so our friend leans over the bridge and watches the patriarch, and speculates as to what will be the best way of putting a fly over him on some future occasion without arousing his suspicions. The patriarch also watches the man;

he knows quite well that the people of his village do not wear hats like that, and though he is not alarmed he is on the alert for anything that may befall. A wax match is the first thing; it falls into the river with a hiss, and the fish makes a dash at it. But he does not actually touch it, for it is only your very young trout that can be deluded in this way; he will try to eat almost anything that falls into the water.

After the wax match has been refused the man on the bridge is sufficiently interested to desire worms, and he gets a bit of stick and digs about in the grass at the side of the road, a tiresome process, which only results in one worm after much digging. This worm he duly throws in to the patriarch, and a surprising thing happens as soon as the worm touches the water another patriarch, even bigger than the first (he looks a good pound) darts out from under the bridge and seizes the offering while the first looks respectfully, albeit hungrily, on. If the man on the bridge is a stranger to the neighbourhood, his first thought will be that the size of the Exe trout has been much underrated, and he will be pleased. Later on he will be disappointed. But if he has been here before he will know those patriarchs well and will not be misled.

After he has loitered on the bridge and strolled about the village for an hour or so, he makes his way back to the inn and unpacks his portmanteau. Then he has his supper, reads a few chapters of *Lorna Doone* before a comfortable fire, for on Exmoor it is chilly at night, even at the end of April, chats for half an hour with his landlord about Exmoor ponies, and other peaceful things, and so goes to bed, where he falls asleep, lulled by the murmur of the brook that runs under his window.

Eight o'clock is quite early enough for a Londoner to breakfast on May Day down here, for it has been almost, if not quite, freezing in the night, and the trout will not begin to rise much before ten. A brace of five ounce trout and a generous dish of eggs and bacon, followed by plenty of home-made bread and jam and cream, are none too much for the appetite of a man who has slept a whole night in Exmoor air and has splashed in a tub of Exmoor water after it. Moreover, he must go on the strength of that meat practically the whole day, because he is anxious to lighten his equipment as much as possible, and his packet of sandwiches will be but small.

There is nothing that increases a man's benevolence so much as the feeling that he has eaten a huge breakfast, and that every particle of it agrees with him; and as our friend stands before the door of the inn clad in Norfolk jacket, knickerbockers, and shooting boots, waiting for his sandwiches, he is ready to exclaim with Tolstoy's pilgrim, 'My blessing fall on this fair world.' In a short time the sandwiches are ready and he puts on his armour, his light creel over his shoulder his landing net slung to his belt and his sombrero hat on his head. His nine foot split-cane rod is already fitted up, his cast has been soaking while he was at breakfast, and he is ready to begin to fish as soon as he reaches the waterside.

As this is his first day's fishing he proposes to go upsteam and fish from the bank, taking it more or less easily. Later on, when he is in better training, he will begin to fish some miles lower down, or will drive across the moor and fish the Barle, and then he will wade; but today he does not want to get over-tired, and he can fish most of the best pools upstream without wading. If he is well advised he will not begin close to the village, but will take the lane leading uphill past the church, and drop down through the copse on to the river about half a mile higher up.

Here, in a slight bend, there is the most delightful pool possible. The stream turns a sudden corner round an old willow, and finds itself six feet deep before it has time to realise it; and thus for two-thirds of the pool there is that slight nebulosity of deep water running swiftly which really gives the honest angler a chance. As a rule, where Exe runs deep it delights to pretend that it is a sheet of glass, which is not good for fishing. At the tail of this pool Nature has providently put a convenient bush standing a little back from the water, and round this a man may very comfortably throw his flies without being seen. To this bush our friend goes, cautiously stooping, until he is kneeling behind it.

On his cast are three flies. He uses a large March Brown with yellow twist as leader, a small Hare's Ear as first dropper and a Blue Upright as second dropper, this last in deference to public opinion in the West Country, which considers no cast complete without it. One is loth to go against public opinion, but in the Exe I have caught four fish with the March Brown and three with the Hare's Ear to every one with the local fly - not that this is conclusive, far from it; it is merely related as an individual experience. It has seemed to me that the large March Brown kills best when there is a good head of water and the smallest pattern of Hare's Ear when the river is very fine, while the Blue Upright has served me well in a sudden evening rise.

Today, however, the river is running a good height, for April has done its share of weeping, and though there may be a touch of east in the wind, its main characteristic is south. The sun is shining, but light clouds here and there give promise of intervals of shade; and altogether it is as good a day for fishing as a reasonable being could desire. Our friend makes the first cast of the season from behind the bush with a due sense of the gravity of the occasion. The first cast of the year is undoubtedly a solemn thing, and it has been the subject of much previous meditation; in his London chambers he has wasted many valuable minutes in considering exactly how he should make it and with what result. The result has seldom been much under a pound. But anticipation, as a rule, has no connection with fact. In this instance the first cast is not entirely successful. The leader reaches the water, it is true, but it is surrounded with what some angling authority calls 'beautiful but useless' coils of gut, and of course, no fish rises at so strange a phenomenon.

At the third cast, however, he is more fortunate, and there is a flash of yellow in the neighbourhood of the second dropper. He strikes and just pricks the fish, or so it seems. But as he makes his next cast he hears a sharp crack in the air behind him. 'Struck too hard,' he murmurs, and pulls his line in hand-over-hand to see the extent of the damage. As he suspected, the second dropper is gone, but he consoles himself with the thought that he is a little out of practice, and that he must expect to strike off a few flies on the first day. He opens his fly book and takes out another Blue Upright, moistening the gut in his mouth before he fastens it to his cast.

Here let it be said that for the Exe and streams like it I prefer flies tied on gut to eyed flies, at any rate for droppers. On the whole they are easier to put on, and I fancy that for wet fly fishing they make less disturbance in the water and have more hooking power, which is specially important in the Exe, where on nine days out of ten the trout are inclined to rise short.

His new dropper fastened, our friend begins to fish again. In a few casts he gets another rise, and this time he succeeds in hooking his fish fairly. It shows splendid sport, and its first rush might be that of a pound fish. However, there are no dangerous stumps in the pool, and it is not long before he lands it in his net, a lovely little trout of some six ounces. Where half pounders are the limit of one's aspirations a fish of six ounces is a decidedly good beginning, and our angler is pleased with himself. As he unhooks his first capture he notices that the hook has fastened in the corner of its mouth, and wonders whether there is anything in the old Exmoor adage that all the fish caught in a day's fishing will be hooked exactly in the same spot. Out of this pool he catches two more fish, one under three ounces (the limit of size which he sets himself), and therefore returned, the other about a quarter of a pound. Then he gets up from his knees and makes his way along the bank to the next pool, well content with his first quarter of an hour.

It is wiser on the whole in this part of the river to reserve one's energies for the best bits of water, and not to attempt to fish everywhere. Indiscriminate fishing pays, perhaps, if the trout are really on the feed, but if they are not it is sheer waste of labour to fish the long shallows. By keeping to the pools one catches more fish in the end, and their average size is bigger. Even in the pools, except after sunset, only the sharp water or ripple at the head and tail will yield much result; but, given favourable conditions, each pool should be good for five or six rises, out of which one may hook one or two fish according to one's skill and luck.

Sometimes it happens that in one pool as many as four sizeable fish will be brought to basket; then for the next mile there may not be a rise, and then one may come upon another pool where they are on the feed. At times the Exe trout appear to be curiously local in their habits; I have known them to be on the feed in every other half mile of water, while in the intermediate stretches they would not look at anything.

Our friend passes on from pool to pool, mostly getting fish too small to keep, but now and then one over the limit, until he reaches a bridge about a mile and a half from the village. Here he is on the same side as the road, which crosses the river at this point, and as the stream is shallow and not very promising he walks along the road until he shall come to some more pools. Presently he finds himself, as it were, in the middle of the moor, which rises straight up from the road.

Hitherto the hill behind him has been covered with fields and trees, but now all signs of cultivation cease for a while, and there stretches out before him a vast expanse of heather and fern with here and there a point of rock standing boldly out, and here and there a patch of vivid green which shows that some spring is trickling down through the moss towards the river. If a man were to step unwarily into that little patch of green he would sink in above his knees, and possibly deeper. I know no more sudden contrast anywhere: one is in the midst of a scene of cultivation and the work of men's hands; one turns a corner, and is suddenly face to face with the moor rising hundreds of feet above.

The moor! There is no word to describe it; its fascination, for all who have fallen under its spell, cannot be expressed by tongue or pen. A man can only gaze and marvel. As a cloud passes over the sun, and the purple slopes grow dark and threatening, he looks hurriedly over his shoulder, expecting to see a thunder cloud coming up the valley, for when the moor frowns there is but one thing that can match it in awfulness, the great steel-grey cloud that comes up against the wind and rumbles in its path. But there is no thunder cloud there, and as he turns round relieved, the sun reappears and he finds the moor smiling once more. Of all colours, purple is the most mysterious, and here it is in its every shade, from the bright hue of monarchy to the darkest of all, that which is so near black that one can imagine Death wearing it on some high festival - for he too is a monarch. And in the foreground close by, in vivid contrast to all those purples, to the green of the swamp and the grey of the rock, there dances up and down in the sunlight a little yellow butterfly.

The first sight of the moor to a man newly come out of London is a thing to linger over, a thing to think about, and so our fisherman decides to have his lunch here reclining at his ease on the mossy bank with his back against a comfortable rock, and to take his fill of gazing while he eats. First though, for he is first a fisherman and afterwards a seer of sights, he empties his basket out on the grass and counts his catch. Ten fish are they, and they average a quarter of a pound, a very fair morning's work for an unambitious man, while for beauty of form and colour they can vie with the moor itself. A marvellous variety of colour too they can show - bright carmine, rich black, and clear brown and yellow - while the main note is a fine gold, a colour for which the Exe fish are notable beyond all of my experience. One of them, however, is very different from his fellows - a long thin, black fish who had his abode in a patch of the dark water-moss, of which I have spoken as being found more in the Barle than in the bright Exe.

As he lies at his ease enjoying his well-earned lunch, thoughts of the beauteous Lorna and the 'girt Jan Ridd' come to him; he would give a king's ransom to see the one and shake the other by the hand; for no one who has the least of poetry in him, lying here by the side of Exe with the moor all round, not ten miles away from the parish of Oare, could doubt for an instant of their reality, or could feel surprised to see the great yeoman appear suddenly over the brow of the hill riding back from Dulverton on his good but uncertain-tempered horse, Kickums, with his long Spanish gun slung behind him. A big Doone or two would also not come amiss, even though they should question the validity of the angler's card of permission to fish, or, so little do they reck of the law, of his licence itself. He is a man of peace, and he would not attempt to argue the matter with the butt-end of his fishing pole. Rather would he give them fair words, and asseverate how much he admired them from what he had heard of them. So might he escape, for even a Doone must be susceptible to flattery.

Thus he meditates for some half hour, but no one comes to disturb his solitude, and at last he remembers that, though the children of the great novelist's fancy will never come to gladden his eyes, yet are there still trout in the Exe, and while there are trout, life is worth living. So he rises and takes up his rod again. For the next mile or two the fishing is very good. The river winds like a serpent, and at every bend there is a pool of surpassing merit. But our friend finds that the trout are not rising so well as they were in the morning, and by five o'clock he has only added four to his basket. One of them, however, is a good half pounder, and he fully sustained the reputation of his race. There is a chain of little pools, four in number, where the river turns twice in a few yards, and he took the March Brown at the head of the top one.

It was evidently not his real home, for he rushed down-stream at once to the bottom pool until he came to the old stump in the middle of it. He was under it before the angler, in hot pursuit, could realise the danger. That is why his feet are wet; he had to wade in up to his knees to grub about under the stump with the handle of his landing net so that he might dislodge the fish. By a miracle he succeeded, and he is as proud of that half pounder in his basket as he has ever been of a trout in his life. In a pool higher up another good fish which he hooked did the same thing, and though the angler waded in even deeper and poked even more vigorously it got off and he was left lamenting. That fish, he maintains, was fully three-quarters of a pound; but it is the angler's privilege to estimate the weight of the fish he did not catch.

At the hour at which the feeble folk in cities are drinking nerve-destroying tea (not that our friend would reject a cup at this moment, for he has worked hard), he is standing on another bridge about four miles from his starting point, debating whether he shall work on farther upstream or turn back again and go over the same water, fishing the pools he has marked as the best. He decides to take the latter course, as he does not feel fresh enough to do justice to new water, but thinks he is still man enough to take some trout out of pools he knows during the evening rise. Therefore he retraces his steps. He does not fish down-stream, it is contrary to all his theories, but he walks down to the bottom of each pool, keeping well away from the river, and fishes up it again.

And now he gets good proof of the sad fact that a man cannot go on fishing for ever, for though the trout appear to be rising well enough he misses fish after fish. This may be partly due to the deceptiveness of the evening rise, but it is still more due to the fact that he is tired, and that his hand has in great measure lost its cunning. The uninitiated do not in the least realise what hard work fishing in a mountain stream is, even when one is not wading; hence come their somewhat contemptuous opinions of fishermen, for they class them all together, whether they fish for trout or roach, as lazy people who stand by a river and catch rheumatism. But, tired though he is, our angler perseveres, and between the bridges he manages to catch another half dozen worth keeping; and thus, when he stands on the first bridge again, he has twenty trout to his credit, besides a good many small ones which he returned.

By this time it is nearly a quarter past seven, and now arises the question whether he shall go on fishing, for he has nearly another hour of daylight, or whether he shall stroll quietly home along the road. By fishing on he might make his basket up to two dozen, but then again, he might not. No, on the whole he thinks he will not fish any more. For the sake of a fish or two it is not worthwhile tiring himself out and losing flies, and possibly temper. He has every reason to be satisfied with his catch, and besides his dinner will be ready for him at a quarter to eight, and he has forgotten the sandwiches as if they had never been. So he leaves the river and follows the road. Another day, when he finds himself with but five fish to show at the same hour, he will doubtless go on desperately so long as he can see, but today he can afford the consolations of philosophy.

His May Day has brought him the two great blessings of mankind, health and happiness, and a third, which partakes of the nature of both, the blissful consciousness that, no matter how large a dinner he eats (and he means to eat as large a dinner as he can), he deserves it and will not regret it. The old Greek poet has warned us to call no man happy until he is dead; but as we watch this man walking gently back to the village with the shadows lengthening from the great hills on either side, his face as contented as a man's can be, we feel that the poet was wrong, and that here is one at least to whom a long May Day has been pure gold without alloy.

CHAPTER EIGHT

The Duffer's Fortnight

It begins somewhere about 1st June - maybe a little earlier, maybe a little later, according to local circumstances and the nature of the season. A warm spell may hasten it a little, though it does not seem so certain that a cold spell will delay it much beyond the date which custom has ordained for its beginning. At any rate, it will probably not delay the duffer, whatever it does to his fortnight and he will be anxiously expecting his opportunity on a given day every year. 'Duffer's fortnight' is not at all a bad name for the mayfly carnival, though it needs a somewhat more elastic interpretation than has usually been given to it. Presumably it was first so called because of an impression that when the mayfly was on, the duffer could show himself an angler. The origin of the expression is lost in the mist of antiquity, so it is unsafe to assert too confidently that it was not so in those days. Perhaps it was so. The veriest bungler may then have been able to fill his creel, and his pockets, and carry the residuum of three pounders slung on a withy twig. We cannot say that it did not happen like that in those good old times, because we simply do not know.

But we can say heartily and with one accord that so far as the present is concerned the true interpretation of 'Duffer's fortnight' is 'the fortnight wherein the angler proves himself a duffer.' You do not carry any residuum of three pounders on withy twigs nowadays. Your pockets can be kept for their

74

proper functions, as receptacles for tobacco, matches, fly boxes and the like and your creel will always have room for a big bunch of marsh marigolds or other trophies with which the fisherman likes to fill up emptiness and at the same time to placate his women-folk at home. After giving many and wonderful proofs of incompetence in one direction, it is pleasant to be able to show signs of abilities in another. To be able to recognise marsh marigolds when one sees them and thereupon to gather of them largely does afford some consolation. 'If I can't catch fish I can, at any rate, appreciate flowers' - that is the sort attitude. Later in the year a habit of seeking such extraneous comfort may be even more useful, as when the meditation runs, 'I don't care much about fish, but I do like mushrooms.' This, however, is a digression.

The mayfly is an extraordinary insect and it produces extraordinary results on, in and about a river. Observing it in its numbers for the first time, you would hazard a guess that a river must be very prolific to stand the drain on its resources that is undoubtedly going to take place. There, on the one hand, are all the trout intent on feeding to such a degree that they hardly take notice of their natural enemy, man, as he stalks along the bank. There, on the other hand, is the whole army of anglers

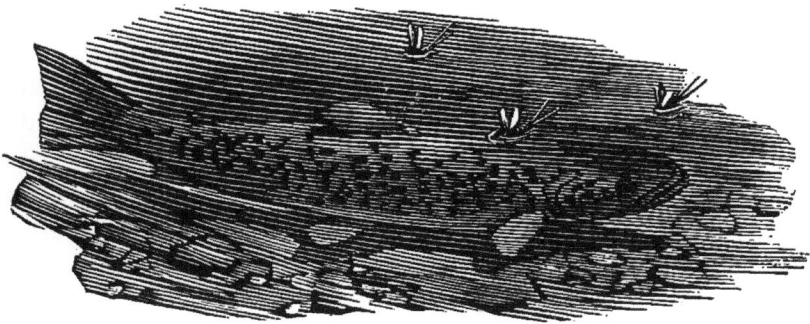

turning out for the destruction of the said trout, armed with every device that can make their victory certain. The contest is surely going to be very unequal and you begin to wonder whether this is sport or a form of butchery. A short Act, *The Trout in Mayfly Time Preservation Act*, occurs to you. Its scope may be gathered from the shorter title which you also think out, *The Ten Brace Act.* Obviously, unless some such provision is made for the future, trout which behave as those trout are behaving in the presence of anglers who look so capable and well equipped as those anglers, are to all intents and purposes an extinct race. Most of us have had some such impression in our time. Some of us even find it recurring year after year when we get the first glimpses of the mayfly rise. But it passes like many other first impressions. There is no better cure for it than to take a rod and begin under the hot sun.

On the whole, the worst feature of the mayfly rise to the disillusioned angler is the remarkable contrast between possibilities and performances. He finds all the big fish, which at other times are just traditions or, at best, dimly-seen shadows, become concrete realities which wallow and splash and surge over the whole stream. They are all feeding or waiting to feed, or taking a hurried interval for digestion so that they can begin again and it looks as though a man could hardly fail to catch as many as he may want. But when he comes to put the matter to the test, he finds that things are not at all what they seem. Most of the fish are bulging, as may be gathered from their restless journeys hither and yon. Of the rest, a good proportion have come to the stage of discrimination and will have even the natural fly just so or not at all. An artificial fly obviously can never be 'just so.'

There remain just a few 'possibles' and the angler's relations with them are commonly as follows: (a) fly pulled away at the critical time and first possible put down; (b) fly seized by a quarter pounder in a bare-faced manner, to second possible's disgust and retreat; (c) and (d) two sixpenny flies left in two three-pound mouths; (e) fly hitched up in tree behind just as fifth possible has made up his mind that he can manage two more and two more only; (f) fly floats beautifully over fine possible of at least four pounds and is taken without hesitation. Battle less strenuous than was expected. Reason apparent later when possible turns out to be one and a quarter pounds, which is a quarter of a pound under the size limit; (g) another sixpenny fly left in another three-pound mouth; and so on.

All this happens amid a scene of general turmoil, which adds to the angler's naturally overwrought condition of mind. Finally, he is reduced to a wild state in which he rushes from place to place and fish to fish, thrashes the unoffending air with his protesting rod and generally does his best to prove that he is indeed a duffer engaged in his fortnight. He returns home in the cool of night with a solitary two pounder, which he caught on a sedge after the mayfly hatch was over for the day and wonders why things should be ordered as they are.

They say - and, of course, many of us know that it is true - that the duffer's fortnight is not all like this. Provided you are able to see the head and body and tail of it, you may get a true mayfly day, a day on which big fish are in the mood and on which you can pick and choose, as is the delightful theory of mayfly fishing and come home with one or two really fine specimens, which you have besieged and conquered in the approved style. You will have nothing to say to two pounders on such a day, for their betters fill your eye, though if you chose you could levy big toll on them. Such days are on record.

Two or three brace averaging four pounds - there have been such baskets and possibly will be again. There are waters where the thing could easily be done with a stroke of luck to help. And there are waters which offer greater inducements to effort even than these, waters where lurk real monsters, hardly seen all the rest of the year except as an occasional wave and a splash under a glittering cascade of small coarse fish fry, but possibly to become surface feeders on one or two days of the duffer's fortnight. The ten pound trout does exist in some rivers and he has been seen feeding on mayflies as heartily as his smaller brothers. But even to get a rise out of him means a waiting game, for he does not come up for the mayfly as a matter of course. The best you can hope for is that he may come up. And if he comes up you may not be able to do anything with him. Still, it is worth a June fortnight even to have watched such a trout feed.

That is the spirit which has animated nearly all my mayfly fishing for years and it explains, if it does not altogether excuse, a very poor total of fish caught in relation to the amount of time and enthusiasm expended. One season, I remember, which I spent on a portion of the Kennet noted for its big fish, yielded almost no trout to me though other rods were getting their three pounders and one got a beauty of over five pounds.

I hardly got a chance of a three pounder that season, the reason being that I spent practically the whole time right at the bottom of the water waiting for my eight pounders to begin to rise. There were eight pounders there - at any rate there was one, for I saw him one day but a few inches from my eyes; I was looking over the camp-sheathing and he was swimming slowly upstream close beside it - but the trouble was that there was no mayfly, or not enough to make the big fish rise. Day after day the appearance of odd flies encouraged a hope that the rise was just about to begin, but day after day it stopped short of the desired point. So I got no sport worth mentioning and never saw one of my eight pounders take a fly.

I have spent other seasons quite as unprofitably, but I have usually succeeded in getting at least one rise out of a fish which has seemed to me worth long waiting. The ambition to get a monster has of course given me some thoroughly dull days, dull at least so far as active employment is concerned. I remember one snatched with difficulty amid the stresses of war-time which almost beat my own record of nothingness.

It differed from previous days of the same kind in that the train of arrival was an hour earlier and that of departure an hour later, with reference to the sun, owing to the new summer time business. The mayfly does not know about summer time, or, if it knows, it is like those valiant Northamptonshire farmers, who were said to have greeted the new measure with contempt and contumely, and does not care.

The day was hot, distempered by fitful, thundery gusts. The available shade was limited to one extremely insufficient willow, hardly big enough to make a cricket stump, let alone a whole bat. This tree, though it did not exactly wither away like the scriptural gourd, was almost equally deceptive because of its immobility. In the morning and the early part of the afternoon it offered a little protection provided I crawled round as the sun's angle altered. Afterwards only by sitting in the river could I put the treelet to any use as a sun filter. You will deduce that I did not do this. But earlier I spent a good many recumbent hours. I was mostly occupied watching insects on and about the water - a wonderful show of fly life. At times my eyes may have closed; I do not remember. Certain it is that there was no occasion for using the rod in spite of all the fly - alder, button, sedges (various and many), olives and their spinners, black gnat in droves, yellow May duns and occasional green drakes. Not a fish more important than a small dace moved to anything.

It was about four o'clock when the mayfly began to hatch, induced thereto by an interval when clouds covered the sun. But the clouds passed, the heat returned and the hatch ceased abruptly. I left the riverside thereupon in quest of some sort of meal to hearten me against the work in prospect when the fly really should come on. I timed the thing well, for the hatch really did begin as I returned. And a very good hatch too. But I cannot say that it made much difference. The dace dimpled a little more freely and may have been a bit bigger, but it was long before I saw a trout, one of those few big ones which the water holds, make any sign of life. So there was still no fishing to speak of. One soon gets tired of spoiling mayflies over dace.

After a while, however, there was a plop from a heavy fish and up he came again in the stream between the two eddies, the place where day dreams had figured the record trout a-rising. Not to waste words, he took at the first fair cast and plunged deep down into the twelve-foot pool, strong as a submarine. The real thing at last! But the triumph ended in a netful of silver scales and red fins - a distressing four-pound chub. And there was a similar triumph a few minutes later - a three-pound disappointment.

Further, there was nothing to record until almost the last moment when a move had to be made upstream in view of the last train for home. Then at a corner (where by the way in the morning was seen a great length of something which head-and-tailed once, but seen from such a distance that it might have been a trick of the imagination), at that corner was evident a feeding fish of great size. And it cruised on a definite beat, up and down, a hopeful sign. It was a long cast and an awkward one owing to a bush and tall rushes, but at last the fly reached the right spot, was taken and - ye gods! - what a moving of the waters! That, alas, was all, for the line came back without the fly. There sad, and so home, as Pepys said when the minikin string broke. A bad end to a poorish day. But it was worthwhile to have had it, if only to see that monster swirl. He may have been another chub of course, a colossus among chub. But I hold that I am entitled to be of different opinion. In fact I must be, in order to justify my attitude towards mayfly fishing in general.

That day was in 1916. I also had a little mayfly fishing in 1917 which I will duly record, since it fits in well with the scheme by which my sport with this fly is ordered under Providence.

At any more normal period I should have made bold to complain a little. I still do not think I was treated well. Providence does things too thoroughly. It began by tantalising me with the sight of a mayfly sitting on a sailorman's white cap in the Baker Street-Waterloo Tube Railway.

I might so easily have been spared that unusual sight. Come to think of it, you might travel the line year in year out for a decade and never see the like again. It was a real live mayfly, not an imitation, which I imagine, would be contrary to the King's Regulations and might be provided for under some comprehensive article. For the insect itself I am sure there is no provision of any kind.

Well, as I say, I saw that sight, had speech with the unconscious wearer of the cap and deduced that the mayfly was up in a district where I should be on Bank Holiday. That, of course, set me to thinking about fishing in spite of much graver preoccupations which then were mine.

For in that district lives what an amusing writer has called 'the occasional trout.' What better opportunity of making the acquaintance of that mysterious but attractive fish? I have a firm conviction that he is never under three pounds, and usually somewhere between seven and ten pounds. To be brief, I laid all my plans for catching him and proved to my own satisfaction at those rehearsals which take place on the edge of sleep that he was certainly a seven-pounder and maybe a bit over. Meanwhile I laboured abundantly so as to have a few hours free during the holiday. How fortunate, I thought, that the district is early in the matter of mayfly.

To condense the story, I succeeded in snatching two evenings. The first was ushered in by a thunderstorm and chased out by another thunderstorm. It was a wretched sandwich of an evening, flattened utterly by the two convulsions on either side of it. Nothing rose which I could honestly claim to be other than dace or bleak. Fly was in evidence, but sparse and dispirited.

The morrow was lovely. It inclined to a fresh wind all day, but as I toiled with papers, that did not worry me. About tea time, moreover, the wind began to drop and my hopes rose. It was going to be one those perfect mayfly evenings which mellow from gold to rose, from rose to opal and from opal to the deep blue of a summer night. I set out across the knee-deep grass, drinking in the goodly scent of the may and thanking a benevolent Providence for a few hours of perfection.

And so I came, leisurely rejoicing, to the river, at whose margin even from a distance I could see the spinners beginning their evening dance.

Thus to the water's edge. I looked down and behold the river was as soup in a tureen! And so it remained till I came sadly home, having seen a magnificent hatch of fly with not a fish paying the smallest attention to it. I learnt afterwards that higher up the valley the thunderstorms of the day before had brought with them floods of rain lasting for hours. Which was an explanation, but no comfort. On the whole this was the poorest mayfly season I have ever had.

In other and better seasons I have had some fine opportunities on first-rate waters, thanks to the kindness of their owners or lessees, but I have never succeeded in doing anything with them worth mentioning. Somehow or other I always make the worst of mayfly opportunities, and the occasional successes, which even I have not been able wholly to avoid, have usually left a regret, *amari aliquid*, behind.

There was one very queer season on the Kennet below Newbury, which started with a deluge, continued with a flood and wound up with a spell of winter. I got to the river on a Saturday morning to find things not wholly inauspicious. Albeit in a close and thundery air the morning hatch of fly was satisfactory and for about half an hour it seemed as though the fish were about to feed in earnest. Two admirable trout, indeed, turned themselves miraculously into chub in the brief space that ensued between hooking and landing, while several plump dace made a mess of several dainty flies which had been dressed for their betters. Then in the distance arose a dark mysterious cloud, which muttered ominously as it approached.

Having been caught in that way before and having recently read warnings as to the 'conducting' properties of fly rods, I retreated without loss of time and presently, safe under cover, was watching a storm of malevolent vehemence which threatened to stop mayfly fishing for the day. It not only threatened, but performed, and by 6 p.m. the river was running pea soup in appalling quantities.

On Sunday it continued thick, only beginning to fine down towards evening; and on Monday, though the river was fairly clear, the wind arose in its might to rob angling of any small chance it might have had. Some small hatch of fly about 2 p.m. there undoubtedly was, but the wind and cold prevented any rise from anything that looked even remotely like a trout and the fly ceased abruptly in about an hour.

Dispirited and shivering but inspired with the doggedness of ill temper, I hung about the river all the rest of the day, waiting for something to turn up. It was quite 8 p.m. before the wind dropped and disclosed a grey, cold river flowing sullenly beneath a grey, cold sky. So cheerless was the prospect that I made a movement for home and supper when 'plop' and again 'plop' caused a hurried return to the river.

Yes, by the powers! there was a great trout feeding close under the camp sheathing, rising with a cheerful abandon begotten of the mayfly season. What he was taking was undiscoverable; nothing was visible on the surface and spent gnats were out of the question; all signs of mayfly had ceased hours before. Still, there he was and he must be tried. He was in an awkward place, just in the eye of a swirling eddy, where the first fly offered was promptly drowned. It was drowned a second time and then taken off to make room for a dry one. This swept down the run, hovered for a second at the eye and was just about to be drowned, too, when 'plop' - the trout had it. There followed a tearing rush straight downstream, through the deep pool, past a bush, over which the twelve-foot rod could just be lifted and on for the swift water and the thick weeds. Here he would be a free fish to a certainty, for there was another bush in the way over which the rod could not be lifted. Therefore it was a case of butt or break. Butt had it, mercifully and he came slowly and doggedly back, fighting deep and trying to get in to the bank. Then all of a sudden he caved in, came to the top, rolled over on his side and so into the net, as pretty a four-pounder as the eye could wish to see, a thought long perhaps for a Kennet fish, but small-headed and thick-shouldered.

Now if Providence had stopped there it would have left me with a completely happy and triumphant memory of a great occasion. My biggest mayfly trout (he weighed four pounds one ounce and I have only caught one other on mayfly which just touched four pounds) would have served me as a perpetual and pleasant reminder of the beauty of 'sticking to it.' But what did Providence do?

It did this. Scarcely was my four pounder on the bank when a few yards higher up there were more 'plops,' and another great trout was hard at it in exactly the same way, feeding vigorously on nothing. He was covered and he rose fair and square, but, alas! a hand, shaking from the recent conflict, had lost its cunning. The response to the rise was too rapid, the fish evidently objected to having the fly pulled away and went down, to rise no more. Marvellous to relate, twenty yards higher up yet a third big fish began to feed almost at once, but there was more excuse for missing him, for he was right under a willow bough and could only be reached by a side flick, in the course of which the line got entangled in the nettles on the bank. Therefore, though he took the fly all right, the rod could not get on term with him and he departed untouched.

Think what a leash it would have been, for the other fish were quite as big as the one I caught! But Providence evidently meant me to suffer the pangs of regret and to make sure of it, sent me to the same spot on the following morning. Then, a few yards lower down, I at once hooked yet another four-pounder, played him for several minutes and was just preparing to use the net, when a voice said 'Hi' or 'Good Morning' or 'Any Sport?' or some other offensive thing, my attention was distracted for a moment and the fly came away. For twopence I would have pushed the owner of the voice into the river. Providence I would have pushed in for nothing at all had I had the chance. I have never had to do with four such big fish in such close succession before or since.

Francis Francis and others used in old days to begin the mayfly season on the Itchen and continue it on the Kennet, thus getting some three weeks of fishing. One season I tried to emulate this achievement and pursued the insect to three different rivers. It was not a great success. Here is the record of the business as I set it down at the time. I leave the confession unaltered as it points a moral or two:

There was a certain piquancy about my first view of the mayfly this year, because it came within a week of my last view of the March brown and I was able to compare the creatures with a freshness of interest that was gratifying. I remember thinking well of the mayfly and disparaging the March brown, because I was sure that the larger and later insect would make ample amends for the scandalous behaviour of the smaller and earlier. Now I want something larger and later still, which shall make good the abominable deficiencies of the mayfly. Not to put too fine a point upon it I should like dragonflies to become trout food all through July and to enable me so to catch something. I badly desire to have some satisfactory standard of comparison by which I may disparage the mayfly thoroughly and reduce it to the level of the yellow May dun which trout do not take. They do not take the mayfly either, of course, not really, but people think they do. I wish to expose that fiction by the aid of a dragonfly carnival and enormous fish safely landed with No.10 hooks. People would know then that the mayfly is not the real thing.

By way of preparation for this, let me with brief dignity relate my experiences. First there was a day on the Surrey stream which of old misled me into the idea that the mayfly was a nonesuch - I apologise for the expression, but it dates from Cavalier-Roundhead days and my mood is Roundheaded. Well, on this Surrey stream I saw such plenty of mayflies as never was before. Usually twelve flies in an hour make you excited and 24 are the cream of the cream. But on 14 May I saw more flies in five minutes that would last half an ordinary day. And the fish ignored them, practically.

The manner of their behaviour was this. Upstream, a hundred yards or so away, at a vague point around a corner, would come a resounding splash and I would hurry thither to await its repetition. Ten minutes would pass and then would come another splash, somewhere near the spot I had left, an indeterminate B., and I would hurry back. Followed more waiting and then a third splash at or about A. Renewed expectancy there would be rewarded by a fourth splash - at B. Why, a man will ask, did I not display presence of mind and remain at B.? I tried that. The result of it would be two and even three splashes at A., which was more than human nature could stand. Also I tried casting at the place where the rises seemed to be, as judged by the ear. And that was more than the trout could stand.

The day yielded me one wretched trout and one indelible disaster. I did at last find a glorious fish feeding persistently, an easy fish, a fish close to my own bank, a five-pounder. He was what, from hearing about other men's sport, I have learnt of late to call a 'sitter.' I fished for him as I imagine those other men do, with no mistake, no drag, no mischance. And he took as those other men's do, felt as heavy as theirs, made my reel scream as theirs - and got off as mine do. Sitters!

Now let me tell of the visit to one of the most charming streams that join the Thames, with one of the best of fellows and hosts that ever cast line. The mayfly had appeared ten days too soon and - was over.

And now let me sing of the Kennet and the Brethren and the seven streams and seventy carriers and seven hundred thousand three pound trout, which all welcomed me in pouring rain. Even as I got there I trembled at the sight, so much was the fly and so furious the rising of the three-pounders. It was a bewildering spectacle to a man who had known trouble. The Brethren as usual were admirably calm and surveyed the scene unmoved. 'When,' they said, 'the rise begins, we'll put him on the Grove.' I was speechless. 'When the rise begins!' 'Isn't,' I presently said feebly, 'isn't this a rise?'

It wasn't. The rise began at two. I saw a great river simply heaving with three-pounders, and naturally my mind became unhinged. I rushed up and down the seven streams and the seventy carriers and the seven hundred thousand three pound trout rushed too; we all rushed. My rod went up and down like a flail, my fly fled hither and thither like a snipe, the sun came out, the sky took on a blue face - it was a mad and merry time. I arrived at the point of tea with a brace weighing just under four pounds and I expect I ought to have had five brace weighing forty.

And then after tea there was the five-pounder to be caught at the point of the island and the four-pounder under the hedge and much more to be crowded into a delirious evening. To reach the five-pounder needed a 22 yard cast, with about five yards of slack over and above to counteract the weed bed and the eddy. But the strength of the insane was upon me and after a strenuous hour I succeeded in losing him. And I lost a three and a half pounder just below him and a three-pounder just below him and the four-pounder under the hedge and had other brave doings worthy of the opportunity and of me. The end of it all was one more fish below the size limit, which had swallowed the fly and made himself bleed. What a day it would have been for a calm, capable person who had not known trouble.

I could tell of another day on a water scarcely less desirable in my eyes, a day spoilt by floods of rain and a thickening of the stream, and of another day when pusillanimous retreat before a storm deprived me of the half hour in which the trout really were on. But what is the use of more ado? How am I to persuade trout to take dragonflies, and so repair my fortunes? That is now become the question.

One more moral and the chapter must come to its close. This is connected with the conditions which prevail on a hard-fished ticket water on which I took a rod one year.

With the mayfly on the wing every single soul who could be on the water, was on the water, which meant a considerable congregation of souls. And that meant what is pleasantly called 'intensive' fishing - that is to say, wherever you happened to be, a brother angler would be within exclamation distance, possibly even within a whisper. Where there are plenty of trout intent on mayfly this does not perhaps seriously affect sport, but still, one prefers a little more elbow room when one can get it, if only because exclamations are not always intended for other ears. Also I still hold, despite sea angling festivals and the like, that angling is of its nature a solitary diversion.

I got out none too early (several experiences on that water ultimately convinced me that to make sure of the rise you should be out with the lark and home with the owl), and I received a delightful surprise on finding myself quite alone on the first stretch I came to, where the smaller river rounds a corner lined by trees on the far bank. This smaller river is not of so much account as the big one and though it holds good fish, it has the reputation of being dour. Besides, it is later than the other and the mayfly was not really due on it yet. It seemed to me that so far it, or at any rate this topmost rather inaccessible, corner, might have been overlooked.

Having evolved this theory, I saw several mayflies and immediately after, poised near the surface, a trout of such calibre as I had not deemed possible in the stream. Then I saw another even bigger, and after him three more, all big and all in evident expectation of the hatch. 'This,' I said to the solitude, is good enough. Here I am; here I remain.' I will not deny that I was excited. To have lighted on a practically virgin piece of water during the mayfly time on one of the hardest flogged fisheries in England was a piece of superb luck, by which I hoped to profit to the tune of three brace weighing at least twelve pounds. Afterwards no doubt the stream would be fished as intensively as the rest, but for the moment I seemed to be not only alone, but also the first to burst into that silent scene.

Let me now confess that the affair did not turn out quite as I had hoped. Those large trout, so visible and apparently so ready for me, displayed an unexpected amount of self-control. I laboured over them for about an hour and the net result was three short rises. It struck me that they could not really be on terms with the mayfly yet and that they might be the better for a rest while I had lunch. One thing was practically certain - they could not fail to come on some time, when the fly should get a bit thicker and then, not having seen any other artificial flies, they would certainly take mine.

So I lunched, sitting peacefully on my basket, with one eye cocked for a proper rise at a fly - so far it had been a matter of occasional bulges after nymphs. To me, thus sitting, entered then he whom I shall call the First Angler, both by reason of his priority and of his acknowledged skill. With him there was a pleasant chat. In the course of it, it appeared that he knew all about the corner. More than that, I learnt that its fishable condition was due to him, for he had recently been among the withies with a pruning knife. The result, easy casting, combined with good cover, did him great credit. But it was evident that I was in no sense a discoverer. Probably, indeed, the good fish which he had lost early that morning was the topmost of my five.

I was still sitting on my basket meditating whether those big trout were, after all, quite the untutored beings I had hoped, when the Second Angler arrived, to take up a watchful position some way lower down. A common boredom (the rise had either petered out or not properly begun) caused us to drift together eventually, and to converse a while. From our talk I gathered that the corner was not only the favourite resort of, but had even been named after, the Second Angler. I became doubly certain that I was not its discoverer.

Presently, the Second Angler having gone downstream, arrived the Third Angler. 'Yes,' he said, 'I had hold of a good one there this morning,' pointing to the spot where No. 2 (of my five big ones) had been displaying his massive charms.

The Third Angler confessed to not being a patient fisherman and departed, after assuring me that the bottom of the water was the best place thus early in the rise. Soon after I went away myself to get some tea, as nothing was doing and the fly had not yet begun.

I stayed away too long. The Fourth Angler, who was hard at work when I came back and who landed two or three fish while I was getting to work again, pointed out the exact spot where he had just lost a four-pounder. The fly must have appeared the moment it caught sight of my departing form, and the Fourth Angler cannot have been long behind it. But the take, such as it was, was over by the time I got back and I saw no more big fish move. My friend's big trout, by the way, was not one of my original five, but a fish some little way below. I knew about him in the morning and had mentally decided on him for the completion of my three brace - he was a worthy fish.

I will now pass hurriedly to the late evening and the Fifth Angler, who was plodding philosophically home. I had left the corner by then and was waiting about for sedges lower down. 'I've only got a brace,' said the Fifth Angler, 'but I had bad luck. I lost three really good fish up at the top under the bushes on my way down in the morning.' So there were the rest of my big ones duly accounted for!

The moral is that a corner may not be so quiet as it seems and that visible big fish are not always as good as in the basket.

CHAPTER NINE

The Evening Rise

The angler is a hopeful mortal who ought to know better, and the evening rise is a delusion based on his weak readiness to believe all good things of the time that is coming; also, there never was a river better named than the Test. If an angler should win through four days on this river (taken when leisure permitted, and in malign consequence when the conditions were uniformly unfavourable) without having his patience tried to the breaking-point, set him down as the angler who is indeed complete. The Itchen has a name full of irritating possibilities, and it does its best to deserve it. But the other has something of solemnity in its designation, as befits a stream whose trout are greater size and whose fascination for the fisherman is so much the more irresistible.

Yet, patience or no patience, an invitation to fish the Test is a thing to accept by telegram, for there are days when the fish rise boldly, and the angler fills his creel with three-pounders - other men have these days, so one is sure of it. Also there is the evening rise; one has this oneself, though it somehow differs from other people's if one may judge from their experiences is always useful, so a description of four varieties of the evening rise witnessed on the Test may not be amiss. The first was nearly at the end of June, after an amazingly hot day, as hot days go in England now. A north-westerly breeze and a conspicuous lack of fly had kept the fish down, except for one or two old stagers that were feeding lazily and safely on black smuts, whose microscopic size forbade imitation. But in the evening the wind dropped, the sky became a glorious expanse of gold and rose as the sun sank, and the rise seemed a moral certainty.

Placed by my friend's kindness at the very best spot on his water, a gliding shallow above the weir on which the three-pounders were wont to dine, I esteemed myself fortunate, and was almost immediately rewarded by seeing a rise. Creeping into a position among some rushes below the fish, I covered him with a medium-sized Blue Dun, which he took without hesitation. But the luck was on his side. Though he was apparently well hooked, and though the line never slackened, the hook came away after his first magnificent rush, and I realized that one three-pounder at least was not mine. I withdrew sadly, and made my way upstream towards a bend where, above a piece of camp-sheathing, a big fish had been spotted in the daytime. The evening light made it possible to see a rise from a long distance, and I soon marked a ring in the desired spot close under my own bank. But, alas! even as I marked it something else claimed attention - a thin veil of mist that seemed to be coming down-stream. I ran, but the mist reached him before I did, and he rose no more. The fatal mist then moved on to spoil the rest of the water, and, though one two-pounder rewarded a desperate race to the shallow below the weir, the evening rise may be said to have ended before it had really begun, and not another trout moved.

The next day was not unlike the first, except that it was not quite so hot and rather more windy. The evening sky was again glorious, but again, just as the fish seemed likely to feed, the mist made an unwelcome appearance. Before it rose, however, I just had time to hook with a big Wickham the trout above the camp-sheathing - and to lose him. It is most depressing to lose a big fish when time is precious; it encourages a fatalistic anticipation of failure which is bad for the basket. Patches of the baleful mist and a total absence of rising fish did not help matters; but there remained one chance - a small side-stream which was really a backwater of the main river. This had a fair evening reputation, and from the distance it seemed as yet to be free from mist. I therefore hurried over the meadow towards the bridge which crossed it. Here, sure enough, were fish rising, and rising well, and a big sedge seemed appropriate to the hour, as several were fluttering about the banks. But the trout would not look at it, though they continued to rise steadily at something invisible. Nor would they move at a Silver Sedge of smaller size, nor at a still smaller Blue Quill. At last in sheer desperation, I put on the smallest Blue Dun in the box, and at once rose and hooked a trout that had refused all the other flies. He fought like a thing possessed, and, though he was only one and a half pounds, he had to be handled judiciously on the tiny hook. Judicious handling means loss of time, and before I had him in the net, the mist was upon us. As a signal, every trout in the stream stopped feeding, and the second evening rise was over.

The third evening rise was experienced a week later, on another side-stream, after a thundery, flyless, fishless day. It consisted of a single dimple, caused by a grayling, and I took full advantage of it and the fish was a fine specimen of two pound six ounces. I believe, however, that the trout rose for half an hour after we had gone - an event for which they were, no doubt, waiting. The keeper said next day that it was quite a pleasure to watch them. The fourth day was again devoted to the main river. The sky was heavy with rain all the morning and afternoon, but about five o'clock it began to clear up, and by 7 p.m. a lovely evening was assured. At last I was to see a real evening rise. It was begun by a good fish under the opposite bank, which came up continuously and voraciously until a small silver sedge floated over him. He then came up no more. I attributed this to my having dropped the fly too close to him, and resolved to be more careful with the next trout, which was rising equally steadily about twenty yards higher up. I covered him with a really excellent cast. The fly dropped as lightly as thistle-down five feet above him, floated directly over his nose without the least suspicion of a drag, and put him down at once.

This convinced me that the Silver Sedge was not the fly, and I changed it for an Olive Quill, which put down a third fish every bit as speedily. A Wickham put down a fourth, and a Black Hackle put down a fifth, while a big Red Sedge put down two at one cast. Then I began to have doubts, and put on a Blue Dun, as what fly was on the water seemed to be of that character. This invaluable pattern put down about a dozen fish with promptitude, and my doubts increased, but there seemed to be no valid reason for changing it. At last I reached the top of my beat - a big pool shelving out on to a perfect shallow. Here numbers of fish were feasting on a splendid batch of duns, which were plainly visible against the sky. My fly was visible, too, and it looked exactly like the naturals. It put down those fish one by one until only about six continued to feed. Five of them were beyond my reach, and one, a monster, seemed to care nothing about my fly. He was rising just on the edge of the rapid at the head of the pool, and the Blue Dun passed over him several times, leaving him unmoved. My friend, who, being a better fisherman than I, had succeeded in putting down all the fish in his own section more quickly, and had come down to watch me, questioned my ability to frighten this fish, but I was not convinced. I looked through my fly-box and found an enormous Red Sedge, built for the Kennet. Then I tied on and cast out, and I am pleased to say it put the monster down at once. After this we went home with the consciousness of something accomplished. But I cannnot speak highly of the evening rise as I found it.

CHAPTER TEN

Hooked and Lost

The angler should beware of those tags of proverbial philosophy which have, insensibly almost, attached themselves to his craft. Chief among them is that fallacious parody which insists in season and out that 'it is better to have hooked and lost than never to have hooked at all.' There is probably no short sentence that has wrought more havoc with many a serene temper than this 'idol of the water-meadow,' as, after the ancient fashion, it might be called.

On the face of it, it seems so reasonable. We do not, one reflects in the study, fish for slaughter; we have no lust for blood; we are contemplative men interested in the way of a trout fly. To have a way with a fly a trout must be alive; the row of corpses on the dish at even is but an accident - a regrettable accident almost, to be endured, since it shows that we have contemplated the day through to some purpose, and because a sordidly material world demands that theory should sometimes be supported with proofs. Dead trout, in short, are proofs, statistics, tables, things wholly alien from the high thinking of our profession; we would just as soon be without them. So reason we at home, in the train and even at the waterside, until reason goes reeling under the first buffet of misfortune.

The account of some typical events on the Itchen may serve to illustrate the futility of proverbial philosophy such as this, begotten of a taste for juggling with words, and nurtured by a habit of compromising with truth. In the morning fate was on the side of error; never a fish would look at anything, though there were rises in plenty and fly in abundance. Olives, reds, blues, gingers, and the shades between were tried conscientiously, but the trout might have all been dead in a dish for the response they gave. The thought arose that 'it is better to have hooked and lost than never to have hooked at all,' and it seemed a good thought. To it succeeded temptation, and old vows, solemnly taken, became of no account. In short, a fly on a 000 hook was knotted to the cast, and, as all dry-fly anglers, save the very few born lucky, know, this is a sure road to hook and to lose. *Ex nihilo nil fit* - 'treble nothings' catch nought.

Oddly enough, however, the first fish that rose at the tiny Blue Upright was caught, and the toy hook was found for once in a way to have taken firm hold. But it was only a small fish, scarcely sizeable, so it went in again. The second fish rose, and was not hooked. The third, a good one, lay under the opposite bank in a wide place and it needed a superhuman cast to reach it. But a puff of wind aided, the fly fell right; the trout rose boldly, and in a moment was tearing downstream. Gradually line was wound in, and the fish manoeuvred across, through a sparse bed of rushes, over weeds and into a clear run under the near side. The folding-net was opened, the rod bent to the final strain, and then the fly came easily away, while the fish remained exhausted just out of reach. 'It is better to have hooked and lost than never...' But the saying seemed inadequate at the moment, and ended in vigorous but irrelevant Saxon.

The next fish was feeding under the near bank and in an easy position. It took the fly like a lamb, gave two kicks, and was also gone. There was a moment of silence, and then,

in a still, small voice came, 'It is better to have hooked...'
But the sentiment faded away at that point. Upstream some
fifty yards, and sheltered from the wind by a spinney, was a
broad shallow, and on it fed five trout, all good ones, and all
within reach from one spot. The first took the Blue Upright
as though it had been waiting for it all day. It ran, jumped,
tumbled, and finally gave in, submitting to be drawn
netwards, a good two-pounder. Then the fly came away as
the net was being lowered to the stream. Again there was a
silence, and again an effort was made to snatch consolation
out of verbiage. 'It is better...' But it was obviously not
better, so nothing further was said in that vein. None of the
other fish on the shallow would look at the Blue Upright, so
several other flies were put over them, flies large and small.

At last a double-hooked Black Midge (warranted to
have hooking powers extraordinary) rose the biggest trout of
the five, held it for a second or two, and came away fatigued.
'It...' began the angler with heroism, but that was the last
word of proverbial philosophy that day; a sentence beginning
with 'it' can finish in so many ways that it is useless to choose
the least appropriate ending, and besides, something had to
be said about the Black Midge before it was taken off. A
Wickham, on a No.1 hook, took its place.

The last fish of the five, being somewhat above the
rest, had not been disturbed by the struggles of its fellows,
and still continued to feed heartily. It was just above a solitary
rush, always a likely position for a free riser, and it took the
Wickham at once, with an eager plunge. At last it seemed that
a decent trout was destined for the creel, for it played deep
and steadily; and then, without warning, that Wickham - that
Wickham on a No. 1 hook - came away just as though it had
been a 'treble nothing'!

And yet there are people who will maintain that 'it is better to have hooked...' But even now the words are too full of bitterness for further iteration.

CHAPTER ELEVEN

Six Days on the Test

' What are you doing, creeping about like a snake in the grass? Why don't you stand up and fish for them like a man?' This was the stern reproof administered by the Test angler of the ancient school who, with his fourteen-foot rod drooping over his shoulder, came upon the rash innovator practising his dry fly subtleties and calisthenics among the sedges. Fascilly Princeps told us this story of old times at dinner a few days ago and we laughed more than a little for we had all been trying with less or still less success to efface ourselves from the landscape the whole torrid day and our chief trouble had been that we were altogether too much like men for the occasion. Even Princeps, who can place his fly to an inch from any point of disadvantage - round a haystack for instance or through a weeping willow - had been compelled to admit that the trout had been hard to approach and some of the rest of us (I venture to speak for the guests) had come to the conclusion that all their spots were supplementary eyes, all their fins nerve centres for the transmission of vibrations to the brain.

When from a really respectful distance, say a hundred yards, you have seen a big trout feeding steadily, when you have fetched a compass of 150 yards to get to a ditch only 60 feet away from him, and when you cautiously put one eye over the reeds which line the said ditch, to find that the fish is put down, what are you to think? Flash of the rod? Tush!

the rod hasn't even been raised. Hat? Forsooth! you should just see my hat - it would drive a scarecrow out of business. Quaking bank? Solid chalk nine times baked. The fact is that we don't know how it happens, merely that it does happen. And we have a lot more to learn both for theory and practice. Some day perhaps one of us will creep up to the edge to find to his disgust that progress is an accomplished fact. I can imagine it - the orthodox dry fly man on his knees to the heterodox object prone among the weeds at the bottom. 'What are you doing wallowing there? Come out of it and fish like a man. You - you eel !'

We had our troubles, plenty of them, during those recent days on the Test, but what compensations there were! With the whole country in the throes of drought, the mere sight of crystal water running along was refreshment. The Test, they said, was lower than it had been for many years, but even so it was a beautiful river with plenty of life and stream. Leaning on the parapet of a bridge one afternoon, I watched the water swirling over stones into a big pool and could almost believe that I was looking at a salmon river which had just fined down into order for a fly. Such an impression is not gained in many places during the drought of 1921.

Even more remarkable than the fact that there was all this water was the behaviour of the fish. It could not be said that they were indifferent to the weather, but they were amazingly cheerful in spite of it. You could feel pretty confident of finding one rising here and there even in the hottest hours, and on most evening there would be quite a brave show of rings for perhaps an hour after about half past nine. There was a curious variation in the time and nature of the rise on different parts of the water. On one beat, for instance, the active period might be from noon to about two while on another it might be from two to four and on another from four to six. Why it should be so I have no idea, unless the presence of trees or depth of water would account for it, but it certainly was the case that nearly everyone had some different report to make at dinner time. Afterwards there was more uniformity, but even the late evenings gave some variety and the blue-winged olive was by no means a certainty everywhere. Some beats had little of it, though they might atone for the deficiency by a fair show of sedges which are happily increasing in numbers on the middle Test again. A few years ago they were sadly falling off.

All things considered, sport was remarkably good and I for one have abundant cause for gratitude, getting, in six days' fishing twenty trout averaging a fraction over 2 lb, besides about a dozen grayling from about 1¼ lb to 2 lb 6 oz. The biggest trout weighed 3 lb 3 oz and the next 2 lb 15 oz. Both were caught on the same day on a small tup and the second was a remarkably deep fish, being only 16¼ inches long with a girth of 12½ inches. When playing him I marvelled how what was apparently not a very big fish, could fight so hard, but his weight in the net soon showed me that I had estimated him wrongly. The three-pounder on the other hand misled me in the other direction, being rather long for his weight. My heart was in my mouth all the time he was on, for I really hoped he might be somewhere near 4 lb. Twice he ran through reeds and twice I had to saw the cast clear of them by hand-lining, a very nervous business. This fight took place during the hottest part of the day with the thermometer not far off ninety in the shade.

The longer I fish the less, I grieve to say, can I make up my mind about flies as a whole, but the evening rise on a chalk stream is not quite so mysterious to me as it was once. The fish are evidently doing certain things which may perhaps be tabulated: 1, smutting or taking oddments; 2, taking spinners; 3, taking (a) Blue-winged olive, or (b) the nymph thereof; 4, taking sedges. My visit to the Test helped me somewhat to a realisation of the importance of stage 3, part b. On most evenings the trout - as we all agreed on comparing experiences - were chiefly occupied with the nymphs and it was really difficult to get them to look at an artificial. One clever angler scored one evening with a Blue Upright. I myself, ringing desperate changes from Orange Quill to blue-winged Olive and back again, could do nothing.

The next evening I tried to profit by his experience and found the Blue Upright of no avail. But on the last evening of all I took a Blue-winged Olive (Halford's pattern of the female) and constructed a sort of nymph out of it by cutting the wings off as close to the body as I could. And with this improvisation I caught a trout at once and was broken by another. So possibly a nymph, maybe the one described by Mr Skues in his latest book, will fill the blank. I shall certainly try it in the future. Stage 3 will then be a time for hurried trial of four patterns: Blue Upright, Nymph, Orange Quill and Blue-winged Olive. With one or other it ought surely to be possible to do the trick. But the chief trouble is finding out in so short and fevered a time which is the right pattern. The temptation to think that 'It didn't quite cover him that time, but he'll have it next cast' is a fearful handicap to resolute changes of fly. I still find myself postponing and postponing till all is over. Half an hour or even three-quarters is not enough for excitable people.

One of the most interesting things in regard to flies which came under my notice was a story related by the keeper. My eyes were fixed, not too amiably, on a bough far above my head on which - somewhere - was sitting my last pink Wickham of the right size. And my friend thereupon told me of another bough to which he had pursued someone else's missing fly. 'And there were six of 'em all in a row like birds on a perch.' The incident is worth adding to the curiosities of tackle-recovery.

CHAPTER TWELVE

A Brace of Tench

The cooing of doves, the hum of bees, and all the pageantry of high summer seem somehow to be recalled by the word 'tench'. Perhaps it is that this fish invites meditation. During the hours, or it may be days, that he has to wait for a bite, even the most unobservant angler can hardly fail to take note of his surroundings. And so the doves and the bees gradually compel a drowsy recognition; the wonderful lights and shades of a July noon first catch and then arrest the eye; a discovery is made that the sky glows with the blue of the south, and that the water is a marvellous and transparent brown; moreover, the insect world moves to and fro, a constant procession of unending activity, and yonder emerald dragon-fly is hovering above the crimson cork that marks the whereabouts of the angler's neglected worm.

A cork float with crimson tip is very necessary to proper angling for tench; it supplies the one touch of colour that is wanting in the landscape, and it is a satisfying thing to look upon. A severely practical mind might argue that it is as visible to the fish as to the fisherman, and might suggest a fragment of porcupine quill as being less ostentatious. But, however one regards it, tench fishing is a lengthy occupation, and must be approached with a leisurely mind. The sordid yearning for bites should not be put in the balance against artistic effect. Besides, it may be said of tench more emphatically than of most other fish: if they are going to feed they are, and if they are not they most certainly are not. As a rule they are not, and their feelings are therefore not so important as the angler's.

In this canal, at any rate, their feelings receive but the scantest consideration. Evening by evening the villagers come forth, each armed with a bean pole, to which are attached a stout window cord, the bung of a beer cask, and a huge hook on the stoutest gimp. A lobworm is affixed to the hook and flung with much force and splashing into some little opening among the weeds, where it remains until night draws down her veil. The villagers sit in a contemplative row under this ancient grey wall, which once enclosed a grange fortressed against unquiet time. But now all is peace, and the cooing of doves in the garden trees has replaced the clash of arms. About once a week the villagers have a bite; a bean pole is lifted by stalwart arms, and a two pound tench is summarily brought to bank; but for the most part the evening's solemn stillness is undisturbed by rude conflict. This is not surprising. Apart from the uncompromising nature of the tackle, there are other reasons against success. The canal is here one solid mass of weed. No barge has passed this way for years, and so there is no object in keeping the channel clear in the summer. If the angler wishes to fish, he must make a clear space for himself with the end of his bean pole. Hence it comes that the villagers angle in two feet of water not more than six feet away from the bank, while the tench live secure out of reach.

The angler from foreign parts (all parts beyond the market town are foreign here) has realised these things, and has endeavoured to strike out a new line for himself. A punt and a long-handled rake were borrowed a day or two ago, and a round pool was cleared among the weeds some twelve yards from the bank, where the water was a good five feet in depth. Further, a narrow channel was cleared between this pool and the bank. Then ground bait, in the shape of innumerable fragments of lobworm, was thrown in, and the tench were left to recover from their surprise, and to find out what a blessing it is to have plenty of good food with plenty of room to eat it in.

The clock on the old tower is just striking four in the grey dawn when he come to prove the value of his theories. There is no row of villagers here now; indeed the world is only just awake, and the earliest of them is hardly rubbing the sleep from his eyes. This is no cause for regret; solitude and tench fishing should be synonymous. Though summer is at its hottest, it is now none too warm, and the dew hangs heavy on the long grass that fringes the canal. But it is just in this cool morning hour, this period of refreshment, that the tench are apt to be on the feed. The angler is equipped with a rod of twenty feet made of East India cane; it is heavier than a roach pole, but it is also much stronger, and was primarily designed for bream fishing in a very deep river. A light but strong silk running-line and a cast of undrawn gut, with one small bullet to cock the float, and a No.7 hook complete the outfit.

The little pool that was cleared yesterday stands out in marked contrast to the weedy surface round it, and it is plainly beyond the reach of any bean pole. With this long rod, however, the bait can be swung out easily enough, and a small lobworm is soon lying on the bottom of the canal ready for the first fish. It is as well in tench fishing to have eighteen inches of gut below the bullet and to plumb the depth so that the bullet itself just touches the bottom. When the float is nicely cocked in the middle of the pool, the angler rests his rod on its pegs, throws a few fragments of worm in round the float, and then takes his seat on the camp stool that he has brought, and composes himself to wait. Tench are not quite so difficult to entice as carp, but where they run big they are not to be hurried. In this canal they run very big; three pounders are occasionally caught by the villagers, and much heavier ones are often seen, and it is these bigger ones that the angler desires; so he is content to wait until breakfast time if need be; it will not be the first occasion.

Presently the sun begins to rise away behind the old wall and the grove of chestnut trees, and the morning grey gradually softens into a kind of luminous opal. Then the

angler sees the first sign of fish; a greenish shadow passes close under the bank almost at his feet. That is a tench of about two pounds, and it seems to have gone out by the artificial channel into the pool. Perhaps it will find and attack the worm waiting there? Anyhow, it is a good sign; it shows that the fish are moving. From time to time a kind of 'plop' may be heard in the middle of the weeds, which also indicates that the tench are breakfasting, but for a long time the bait remains untouched. At last, just when the angler is deliberating whether it would not be wise to put on a fresh worm, the float moves a little uneasily. Then there is a pause, and it looks as if the fish has left the bait. But no, the float stirs again, once, twice, and then begins to sail slowly off.

The angler picks up his rod without hurry, for it is wise to give a tench plenty of time, and strikes gently. There is no mistake about the fish now, and the rod bends handsomely to the encounter. The tench fights very gamely, and does all it knows to bury itself in the weeds round the little pool; but the tackle is strong, and a little extra strain stops it short of them at each rush. The fish plays deep and with great power, but there is no mad plunge such as a trout would give, and at length it is drawn through the channel within reach of the net, and safely landed. It looks very handsome in the morning light, with its armour of tiny scales gleaming in dusky gold, and it weighs a full two and a half pounds.

A nice fish, but not one of the big ones, and so the hook is rebaited and swung out again without loss of time. Then follows another period of inaction, during which the sun gathers power and height, and gives promise of another piping hot day. About half past six the float stirs again, and presently glides off as it did before. The angler strikes and is fast in a second tench. But this time there is no holding the fish, which moves irresistibly across the pool into the weeds opposite. The line is kept tight in the hope of bringing it out again, but it soon becomes apparent either that the tench is curiously inactive or that, in some way understood by fish but never intelligible to men, it has transferred the hook from its mouth to the toughest piece of weed it can find. And so it proves. Much pulling in different directions has no result, and at last the hook-link breaks.

That fish, the angler reflects ruefully, as he puts on a new hook, was undoubtedly a four-pounder at the least. The strain he applied would have turned anything smaller, and it is doubtful whether another big one will bite, for the sun is now on the water. However, there is still an hour and a half before breakfast, so the float and a new hook are swung out once more. Oddly enough, there is a bite at once, and a tench of about the same size as the first is soon in the net, and ultimately in the basket. But this is the end of the morning's sport, and for fully an hour the bait lies absolutely unheeded, and at last the angler winds in his line and departs. His bag of fish is not remarkable, and three bites in four hours and a half do not sound exciting; but he has acquired a noble appetite, and is by no means dissatisfied. Other mornings there are, and plenty of them, when he will not get a fish at all. And again (for such is the glorious uncertainty of tench) there may come a day when he must get assistance to carry home his catch.

CHAPTER THIRTEEN

The Big Carp

For practical purposes there are big carp and small carp. The latter you may sometimes hope to catch without too great a strain on your capacities. The former - well, men have been known to catch them and there are just a few anglers who have caught a good many. I myself have caught one and I will make bold to repeat the tale of the adventure as it was told in *The Field* of 1 July, 1911. The narrative contains most of what I know concerning the capture of big carp. The most important thing in it is the value which it shows to reside in a modicum of good luck. So far as my experience goes, it is certain that good luck is the most vital part of the equipment of him who would seek to slay big carp. For some men I admit the usefulness of skill and pertinacity; for myself, I take my stand entirely on luck. To the novice I would say: 'Cultivate your luck. Prop it up with omens and signs of good purport. Watch for magpies on your path. Form the habit of avoiding old women who squint. Throw salt over your left shoulder. Touch wood with the forefinger of your right hand whenever you are not doing anything else. Be on friendly terms with a black cat. Turn your money under the new moon. Walk round ladders. Don't start on a Friday. Stir the materials for Christmas pudding and wish. Perform all other such rites as you know or hear of. These things are important in carp fishing.'

And so to my story:

I had intended to begin this story in a much more subtle fashion and only by slow degrees to divulge the purport of it, delaying the finale as long as possible, until it should burst upon a bewildered world like the last crashing bars of the 1812 Overture. But I find that, like Ennius (though without his justification for a somewhat assured proceeding), *volito vivus per ora virum.* Now that a considerable section of the daily Press has taken cognisance of the event, it is no good my delaying the modest confession that I have caught a large carp. It is true. But it is a slight exaggeration to state that the said carp was decorated with a golden ring bearing the words, '*Me Valde dilexit atque ornavit propter immensitatem meam Isaacchius Walton, anno Domini MDCLIII*'. Nor was it the weightiest carp ever taken. Nor was it the weightiest carp of the present season. Nor was it the weightiest carp of 24 June. Nor did I deserve it. But enough of negation. Let me tell the story, which will explain the whole of it.

To begin with, I very nearly did not go at all, because it rained furiously most of the morning. To continue, when towards noon the face of the heavens showed signs of clearness and my mind swiftly made itself up that I would go after all, I carefully disentangled the sturdy rod and the strong line, the triangle hooks and the other matters that had been prepared the evening before and started armed with roach tackle. The loss of half a day had told me that it was vain to think of big carp. You cannot, of course, fish for big carp in half a day. It takes a month. So subtle are these fishes that you have to proceed with the utmost precaution. In the first week, having made ready your tackle and plumbed the depth, you build yourself a wattled screen, behind which you may take cover. By the second week the fish should have grown accustomed to this and you begin to throw-in groundbait composed of bread, bran, biscuits, peas, beans, strawberries, rice, pearl barley, aniseed cake, worms, gentles, banana and potato. This groundbaiting must not be overdone. Half a pint on alternate evenings is as much as can safely be employed in this second week. With the third week less caution is necessary, because by now the carp will be less mindful of the adage concerning those who come bearing gifts. You may bear gifts daily and the carp will, it is to be hoped, in a manner of speaking, look these gifts in the mouth - as carp should. Now, with the fourth week comes the critical time. All is very soon to be put to the test.

On Monday you lean your rod (it is ready put up, you remember) on the wattled fence so that its top projects 18 inches over the water. On Tuesday you creep up and push it gently, so that the 18 inches become 4 feet. The carp, we hope, simply think that it is a piece of the screen growing well and take no alarm. On Wednesday, Thursday and Friday you employ the final and great ruse. This is to place your line (the depth has already been plumbed, of course) gently in the water, the bullet just touching the bottom so that the float cocks and the 2 feet of gut which lie on the bottom beyond it terminating with a bait in which is no fraudful hook. This so that the carp

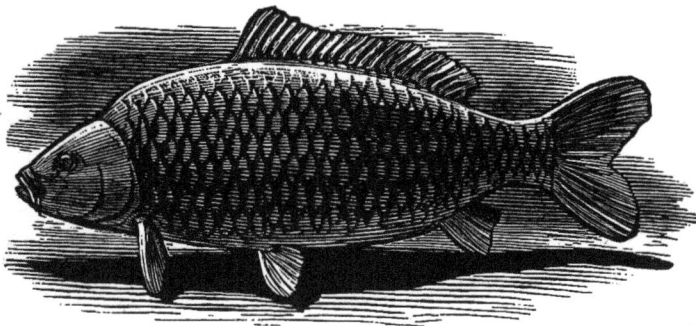

may imagine that it is just a whim of the lavish person behind the screen (be sure they know you are there all the time) to tie food to some fibrous yet innocuous substance. And at last, on Saturday, the 31st of the month, you fall to angling, while the morning mists are still disputing with the shades of night. Now there is a hook within the honey paste and woe betide any carp which loses its head. But no carp does lose its head until the shades of night are disputing with the mists of evening. Then, from your post of observation (50 yards behind the screen), you hear a click, click, which tells you that your reel revolves. A carp has made off with the bait, drawn out the 5 yards of line coiled carefully on the ground and may now be struck. So you hasten up and strike. There is a monstrous pull at the rod point, something pursues a headlong course into the unknown depths and after a few thrilling seconds there is a jar, a slackness of line and you wind up sorrowfully. You are broken and so home.

I mention these things by way of explaining why I had never before caught a really big carp and also why I do not deserve one now. As I have said, I took with me to Cheshunt Lower Reservoir roach tackle, a tin of small worms and an intention to try for perch, with just a faint hope of tench. The natural condition of the water is weed, the accumulated growth of long years. When I visited it for the first time some eight years ago I could see nothing but weed and that was in mid winter. Now, however, the Highbury Anglers, who have rented the reservoir, have done wonders towards making it fishable. A good part of the upper end is clear and elsewhere there are pitches cut out which make excellent feeding grounds for fish and angling grounds for men. Prospecting, I soon came to the forked sticks, which have a satisfying significance to the groundbait-less angler. Someone else has been there before and the newcomer may perchance reap the benefit of another man's sowing. So I sat me down on an empty box thoughtfully provided and began to angle. It is curious how great, in enclosed waters especially, is the affinity between small worms and small perch. For two hours I struggled to teach a shoal of small perch that hooks pull them distressfully out of the water. It was in vain. Walton must have based his 'wicked of the world' illustration on the ways of small perch. I had returned about twenty and was gloomily observing my float begin to bob again when a cheery voice, that of Mr R. G. Woodruff, behind me observed that I ought to catch something in that swim. I had certainly fulfilled the obligation; but it dawned on me that he was not speaking of small perch and then that my rod was resting on the forked stick and myself on the wooden box of the Hon. Sec. of the Anglers' Association. He almost used force to make me stay where I was, but who was I to occupy a place carefully baited for carp and what were my insufficient rod and flimsy line that they should offer battle to 10 pounders? Besides, there was tea waiting for me and I had had enough of small perch.

So I made way for the rightful owner of the pitch, but not before he had given me good store of big lob worms and also earnest advice at any rate to try for carp with them, roach rod or no roach rod. He told me of a terrible battle of the evening before, when a monster took his worm in the dark and also his cast and hook. Whether it travelled north or south he could hardly tell in the gloom, but it travelled far and successfully. He hoped that after the rain there might be a chance of a fish that evening. Finally, I was so far persuaded that during tea I looked out a strong cast and a perch hook on fairly stout gut and soaked them in the teapot till they were stained a light brown. Then, acquiring a loaf of bread by good fortune, I set out to fish. There were plenty of other forked sticks here and there which showed where other members had been fishing and I finally decided on a pitch at the lower end, which I remembered from the winter as having been the scene of an encounter with a biggish pike that got off after a considerable fight. There, with a background of trees and bushes, some of whose branches made handling a 14 foot rod rather difficult, it is possible to sit quiet and fairly inconspicuous. And there accordingly I sat for three hours and a quarter, watching a float which only moved two or three times when a small perch pulled the tail of the lobworm and occupying myself otherwise by making pellets of paste and throwing them out as ground bait.

Though fine, it was a decidedly cold evening, with a high wind; but this hardly affected the water, which is entirely surrounded by a high bank and a belt of trees. Nor was there much to occupy attention except when a great fish would roll over in the weeds far out, obviously one of the big carp, but 100 yards away. An occasional moorhen and a few rings made by small roach were the only other signs of life. The black tip of my float about 8 yards away, in the dearth of other interests, began to have an almost hypnotizing influence. A little after half past eight this tip trembled and then disappeared and so intent was I on looking at it that my first thought was a mild wonder as to why it did that. Then the coiled line began to go through the rings and I realized that here was a bite. Rod in hand, I waited till the line drew taut and struck gently. Then things became confused. It was as though some submarine suddenly shot out into the lake. The water was about 6 feet deep, and the fish must have been near the bottom, but he made a most impressive wave as he dashed straight into the weeds about 20 yards away and buried himself some 10 yards deep in them. 'And so home,' I murmured to myself, or words of like significance, for I saw not the faintest chance of getting a big fish out with a roach rod and a fine line. After a little thought, I decided to try hand-lining, as one does for trout and, getting hold of the line - with some difficulty, because the trees prevented the rod point going far back - I proceeded to feel for the fish with my hand. At first there was no response; the anchorage seemed immovable.

Then I thrilled to a movement at the other end of the line, which gradually increased until the fish was on the run again, pushing the weeds aside as he went, but carrying a great streamer or two with him on the line. His run ended, as had the first, in another weed patch and twice after that he seemed to have found safety in the same way. Yet each time hand-lining was efficacious and eventually I got him out into the strip of clear water, where the fight was an easier affair, though by no means won. It took, I suppose, from fifteen to twenty minutes before I saw a big bronze side turn over and was able to get about half the fish into my absurdly small net. Luckily, by this time he had no kick left in him and I dragged him safely up the bank and fell upon him. What he weighed I had no idea, but I put him at about 12 pounds, with a humble hope that he might be more. At any rate, he had made a fight that would have been considered very fair in a 12 pound salmon, the power of his runs being certainly no less and the pace of them quite as great. On the tackle I was using, however, a salmon would have fought longer.

The fish knocked on the head, I was satisfied, packed up my tackle and went off to see what the other angler had done. So far he had not had a bite, but he meant to go on as long as he could see and hoped to meet me at the train. He did not do so, for a very good reason: he was at about that moment engaged in a grim battle in the darkness with a fish that proved ultimately to be 1 ounce heavier than mine, which weighed on the scales at the keeper's cottage, was 16 pounds 5 ounces. As I owe him my fish, because it was by his advice I put on the strong cast and the bait was one of his lobworms, he might fairly claim the brace. And he would deserve them, because he is a real carp fisher and has taken great pains to bring about his success. For myself - well, luck attends the undeserving now and then. One of them has the grace to be thankful.

CHAPTER FOURTEEN

In Praise of Chub

Much water has eddied under the bridges, foamed over the weirs, and lost itself in the Severn sea since first I came under the spell. But the water must flow longer and stronger yet to wash away recollection of that solemn time. It was high summer on Shakespeare's stream, and afternoon - poetically, it was always afternoon in a lotus-land where white canvas alone shut out the stars of night, but on this occasion prosaically also, for luncheon was over and done with - when from afar I first espied loggerhead basking at ease just outside the spreading willow. No novice was I at the sport of angling, but had taken as many brave fish as most boys of my years, with now and again a pounder among them, while I boasted acquaintance with a veteran angler who had that summer slain a cheven of full two pounds.

But here was something which passed my experience - a chub of unparalleled magnitude in a land where the community spoke with respect of pounders. He had length, breadth, and dignity; he lay at the surface an imposing bulk, and for a while I stood spellbound. Then the natural boy asserted itself, and sought a plan of campaign. Now you must know that cheven is, in some respects, the wisest of fishes, and when he suns himself at the top he is impatient of intruders. But a glimpse of Piscator or of the angle-rod outlined against the sky, and he is gone, sunk quietly out of sight and reach. Strategy, therefore, demands that Piscator should grovel, trailing the angle-rod behind, into some concealed position, whence the fly may be artfully despatched.

Like the earth-worm, I wriggled down the grassy slope to the little bush which offered the only bit of cover on the bank, and peeping round it, found to my relief that loggerhead was still in view. But he was a plaguy long way off - twenty yards at least - and even had I been able to cast so far with the little nine-foot rod - 'suitable to youths' - and the light line, there was the rising ground behind to frustrate me. There was nothing for it but to wait in the hope that the fish might come a little nearer. So I waited, and I will not say that a prayer was not breathed to Poseidon that he should send loggerhead towards my bank.

A long time I waited - maybe half an hour or more - and the fish never moved more than an inch or two, but at long last he seemed to wake up. Some trifle of a fly attracted his attention, and I saw capacious jaws open and shut, and afterwards he seemed anxious for more, for he began to cruise slowly about. Then by slow degrees the circles of his course widened, until finally he was within about twelve yards of my bank. Now I judged, was the time, and with a mighty effort and heart in mouth I switched out the fly at the end of my line (an artificial bluebottle, I remember) as far as I could. It fell quite a yard short, but that mattered little. Round he came sharply to see what had happened. Steadily he swam up to the bluebottle, boldly he opened his mouth, and then I drank indeed the delight of battle. Three pounds he weighed all but an ounce, which doesn't matter, and for quite a time I fondly preserved his skin, adequately peppered and salted, as I thought, but in the end elders and betters intervened with forcible remarks about nuisances. So I was left with his memory only, of which nobody could rob me.

From that day I have revered the chub, and so often as the hot summer days come round (there are not so many of them as there were when Plancus was Consul), so often do I bethink me of the sunlit waters, the cool willow shades, the fresh scent of waterweeds from the weir, the hum of bees, and above all, the dark forms lying on the surface ready for the fly. Some there are who will give you hard words concerning the chub, having, maybe, hooked him on Wye just in the V of the currents where they fondly expected a salmon, having perchance frayed the gossamer trout-cast all to tatters in keeping his brute strength out of the roots, and having disturbed twenty good yards of water to boot. But these unfortunates (I grant them the title) have encountered cheven out of his proper sphere, and their sympathies are warped thereby. Heed them not, but seek him in his rightful rivers, slow-flowing, rush-lined, lily-crowned, girt with willows and rich pastures; take with you your stoutest single-handed fly rod, strong gut, and big palmer flies, or Coachman, Alder, Zulu - it matters little so the mouthful be big and so it have a small cunning tail of white kid; go warily along the bank with eye alert for a dark form under yon clay bank, in that little round hole among the lilies, beneath that tree, above that old log - anywhere, in fact, where a worthy fish may combine ease with dignity and, possibly, nutriment. Having found him, pitch your fly at him with as much tumult as you please; if he does not see you, two to one he will rise. If he does see you or the rod he is gone, and herein lies most of the fascination of it. A stiff neck and a proud stomach are of no use to the chub-fisher, who must stoop if he wishes to conquer.

With good luck you should catch a three-pounder, among others, with very good luck a four-pounder. Those who are what Horace Walpole, I believe, called serendipitous catch a five- pounder now and again. The favoured of the gods get a six-pounder once in their lives. And one or two anglers, for whose benefit the whole cosmic scheme has evidently been arranged, have killed a seven-pounder. But this last prodigy does not, I fancy, reward fly-fishing, though I once - but the memory is too bitter to be evoked. Cheese paste is the thing for seven-pounders if you know of any such, and you can put a piece on the hook of your fly if you like. But you cannot throw it very far, the fishing is difficult, and I much doubt whether they are seven-pounders. Your basking chub is so imposing that one's estimate of his ounces is insensibly coloured by awe.

I have ever been curious to know how big was the chub which Walton and his pupil gave to Maudlin the milkmaid. The only indication vouchsafed to us is that it was 'just such another' as the first one, with a white spot on its tail, and that was the biggest of twenty - all lying together in one hole. From this slender store of evidence I deduce it to have been two and a half pounds, because that is commonly the doyen in so numerous a shoal. The monsters do not often crowd so close as a score together. Four and five pounders are, I think, to be observed four or five in company, not more. How it may be with seven-pounders I know not; likely they swim in pairs, a pair to a mile of river, and that the best mile. I do not know of a pair, but I know of one which a good friend of mine captured in a recent year. It weighed seven pounds and a quarter, and constituted the gravest angling tragedy which has come under my notice in a decade, for the month was May, and my friend is a very honest man. So the monster was gently returned, and some day will no doubt be the father of all the chub.

Loggerhead is a noble, pleasant fish, of thoughtful habit, and he gives right good sport to those who seek him with discretion, but he has, they say, his weak points. On the table - yet is this an angler's matter? All that concerns Piscator in the treatise of culinary wisdom is surely the first injunction, 'First catch him.' Caught, I have never found him otherwise than welcome to the descendants of sweet-throated Maudlin. It needs to inquire no further.

The finest sport I have ever had with chub was on a kind of April day set by accident in the middle of August. The wind blew with a certain amount of vehemence from the south-west; it was none too warm, and the lights and shadows caused by alternation of sunshine and cloud were far more suggestive of spring than of summer. It would have been an excellent day for trout, but it hardly promised great sport with chub. Still, the fortnight of August that had preceded this April day had provided no chub weather worth mentioning. What sun there had been was of pale and watery complexion, with great cloud-banks hovering near, ready to obscure him if he showed any sign of cheerfulness at all. The wind also had been cold and violent, and fly-fishing had been a mockery.

The April day, therefore, was at least an improvement, and the split-cane rod was put together with more cheerfulness of spirit. It would not be a case of stalking fish scientifically, for they would hardly be on the surface; but there was a chance that a big fly thrown into likely spots might bring up a brace or two of decent chub, and give the angler something to show for his pains. In these incredulous days it is sadly necessary to have something to show, and I was growing a little tired of explaining to the lay mind that success cannot be commanded when the weather is unpropitious. Besides, it is thankless work giving explanations that are obviously misunderstood.

Accordingly I was resolute to catch something when I reached the bridge that spanned the Thames - here a mere infant river - with two small arches.

Under the bridge the stream rippled in a manner provokingly suggestive of trout; but though there is much water that might well hold a head of fario in the topmost reaches of the river, the head of fario is conspicuously wanting. A trout has occasionally been taken as high as this, but Lechlade, a good deal lower down, is the first point where the fish becomes a calculable possibility. Beyond regretting this fact, therefore, I took no thought of trout, but looked upstream for a sign of rising chub. Above the sharp water at the bridge is a long, quiet pool, and in its lower corner, on the left bank, is a clump of bushes growing right down into the water, and forming a splendid harbour. A rise was soon seen just below the bushes, and then another, and presently it became evident that the fish were moving. Leaving the bridge, I got into the meadow opposite, from which it was possible to attain a small strip of shingle below, and within casting distance of the bushes. Before the edge was approached, however, some twenty yards of line were pulled off the reel and anointed with deer's fat. Since the chub were rising, they might just as well be attacked with a dry fly. This is, perhaps, an unnecessary refinement for chub; and indeed, it is not by any means always that they will take a floating fly properly, but when they do the sport is not to be despised.

Preparations complete, and a biggish Coachman oiled and attached to a cast that tapered to the finest undrawn gut, the river was approached, and the attack begun. The strip of shingle was about fifteen yards from the last bush, and the distance was soon found. Then the fly dropped close to the submerged twigs. There was no delay on the part of the chub, for a heavy fish plunged at the Coachman the instant it touched the water. So sudden was the response that the line was not released by the fingers holding it against the rod-butt, and a vigorous strike proved too much for the gut. Another plunge, and the chub was gone with the Coachman.

This was vexatious, for the loss of a fish that has been hooked generally frightens the shoal. The rule is not quite invariable, however, so another fly was put on and cast a little higher up, in the hope that the other chub might not have noticed the little contretemps. This seemed to be the case, for a rise followed immediately. There was no mistake about the strike this time, and the reel screamed as the hook went home, continuing to scream as the fish dashed off. A chub's first rush is formidable, and with fine gut it is no good trying to stop it; but if the fish does not break, then it ought to be landed safely and speedily. Before long the fight was over, and a fish of one and a half pounds was in the net, tapped on the head, and thrown out into the meadow, where the creel had been left.

Then the fly was again thrown towards the bushes. Another fish took it immediately, and was landed in the same manner as the first, to which it might have been a twin brother. Then two smaller ones, of about one and a quarter pounds, each came to the net, and were returned. In a good chub river nothing under one and a half pounds is really worth keeping, unless local taste in the matter of fish-diet is very responsive; but big chub will sometimes find grateful recipients in the country, as will be seen. After the brace of small ones had been returned a two-pounder was landed, and after that several more fish of about one and a half pounds. By the end of half an hour there must have been a dozen or more on the bank, and the sport showed no sign of slackening.

Another two-pounder was just in the net when an exclamation was heard from the bridge. A cyclist had paused to look on, and was much impressed with the sight of somebody actually catching something. 'What a beauty,' he said, as the chub was thrown out into the meadow after the rest. This remark suggested that a heaven-sent opportunity was at hand. 'Would you care about some fish?' I asked guilelessly. The cyclist nodded with strange enthusiasm, and was warmly pressed to help himself. He clambered down over the wall with his mackintosh cape, into which he packed the fish with some grass. He was full of gratitude at being told to take them all, and departed, bearing some twenty pounds of chub at his saddle-bow, and leaving me to reflect that appreciation of true merit is hard to find, but when found, pleasant to contemplate.

After he had gone fishing was resumed. A fish plunged at the Coachman, but would not take it. It was so obviously bigger than anything caught so far that it seemed worthwhile to change the fly, and several patterns were tried in vain. At last a wet fly, a big Alder, with a wash-leather tail, was put on, and cast in with a plop just where the fish had risen. A wave came out from the bushes at once, the line tightened, and a gentle strike fastened the hook into something better worth catching. The fish showed plenty of fight, but after one rush under the twigs, from which a steady strain brought it out, there was no real danger, and before long a plump three-pounder was landed. He was deemed worthy of a place in the big creel, and was accordingly killed and put in. After this, sport with the wet fly was quite as brisk as it had been with the Coachman, and the fish were bigger: nothing under two pounds, and the biggest weighing three and a half pounds. To sum up, by the time the rise was over the twenty-two-pound creel was full to the brim, and half a dozen chub beside had to be carried home on a withy twig. All these fish, weighing, with those given away, at least fifty pounds, had been caught without moving from the strip of shingle, and without fishing more than fifteen yards of water, which only shows how chub may be caught when they are really on the feed. The last cast provoked a curious conclusion to a wonderful morning. A fish followed the fly just like a chub, took it, and was played to the net, when it proved to be a small pike of about two and a half pounds. It gave a last kick as the net was about to receive it, the frayed gut parted, and the fly which had caught so many fish vanished for ever.

CHAPTER FIFTEEN

The Float

Were one setting out to construct a philosophy of angling it would be proper, I think, to begin with the float, the link which connects the contemplative man with the wonders of the deep. Everybody knows about floats; even the Philistine uses them to support his inaccuracies touching the craft and the brethren. A sound scholar, from whom I was privileged to receive the rudiments of humane letters, a man decidedly of opinion that fishing, for small boys, was an undesirable species of 'loafing', used, I remember, to be particularly severe about the float; it was unfortunate, perhaps, that the word lent itself so kindly to alliteration, for your sound scholar dearly loves a phrase, and if he be a masterful man, is apt to make it not only define a situation but also determine a policy. Happily there were more ways than one out of the school demesne, and the river bank offered several secluded nooks to which the eye of authority never penetrated.

The float of those days was a fat, globular thing, gross in aspect, clumsy in movement and, though its painted cheeks were not unpleasing to the eye, so far as a float ever can legitimately be condemned as a symbol of folly, it could. Even in that halcyon time when fish were still unsuspicious it needed at least a perch to pull its unwieldy form under; a roach no more than made it wobble. Had the sound scholar based his imputations on the ground of using, not a float, but *such* a float, I should not now be protesting.

For I readily admit that virtue lies almost wholly in having the right float. Shape is important, and so is colour, and it is pleasant at times to dally with material. I have heard many learned disputations on the respective merits of quills from different birds, one man favouring swan, another goose, a third peacock, and each maintaining his opinion with epic accounts of past sport. But as a rule these disputants are a shade too practical; their floats are for use only, and they make no allowance for the element of beauty which should have its place in the consideration.

I used at one time prodigiously to admire a certain slender kind of float fashioned cunningly out of twin sections of clear quill, amber-varnished, silk-lapped, and tipped at either end with a slim point of bone. I lavished a good shilling thereon (you can buy an admirable cork float for the half of that sum), partly out of respect for the ideal, partly from belief in the efficacy of the lovely object in pursuit of roaches. Certainly it rode the stream in dainty fashion, peeping shyly out like some modest naiad, and responding even to that bite, perceived by the men of Lea alone, when a fat old roach makes a round mouth at the bait and sucks it in only that he may expel it the more emphatically, as a peashooter expels a pea. Out of the water, too, that float was a delight; it was pleasant merely to let it hang in the air and to see the sunlight captured in its transparent body. Once we had some really great fishing together. It was a glorious August day, and the roach were on the feed in every hole of the backwater, which was a string of holes separated by short gravel shallows. With no more than a loose handful of groundbait scattered broadcast in each hole, and with a good large piece of white paste on the hook, we caught roach literally as fast as we could. The water was a clear brown,

and it was most fascinating to see down in the depths the gleam of a broad side as the rod went up and the hook went home, and afterwards to be able to follow every moment of the fighting fish. The man who has not yet played a good roach on gossamer tackle in eight or ten feet of really clear water with the sun on it has a rare pleasure still to come. The roach that day were beauties, and of the twenty kept three would have weighed two pounds apiece had I trusted to instinct and not to a spring balance which had neither heart nor soul, and was (I maintain it) rusty somewhere inside.

It was shortly after that day that the naiad float disappointed me by parting asunder at the junction of the two sections of quill, and leaving me floatless just as the fish were beginning to bite. The sections could be joined together again, but the float was never the same after. Sooner or later the water would leak in, and the naiad ceased to be a float, becoming a thing of no classification unless it belonged to the order of plummets. On the whole I prefer my plummets to be of lead, so I gave up the naiad float with a sigh of regret as a last tribute to its beauty. There remains, however, a certain habit of mind induced by it, and I still strive after floats which are good to look at both in line and colour. A slender body of cork on a porcupine quill can be very gratifying. For colours give me scarlet above and green below, with a little knob of sealing-wax at the top of the quill. This last is for use as well as ornament. The uninitiated might suppose that nothing could well be more visible to the angler than the quill's natural white tip sticking out of the water, but what with the dazzle of sun and flicker of wavelets it is often very hard to see, and it is surprising how the little red knob helps the eye. Also, with its aid one can gauge a bite very nicely. Properly poised, there is half an inch above water, and the half of this is white, the half red. When the white has disappeared you have a noble bite as roach bites go, and you may strike at once. It is not often that the roach of these degenerate days take one's float right down and out of sight. For evening fishing, when the last faint light is on the water, a black-headed float is most visible.

At one time I used to fish occasionally through the dark hours, and I was mightily puzzled to find a float which I could see at all after dark. I tried adding a cone of white paper to the tip, and at first deluded myself into the idea that it was visible; but when, after intently watching it for a long time, I discovered that I was really gazing at nothing, I gave it up. The discovery was due to a horrid eel, which had taken my float off in a wholly opposite direction. Incidentally that eel very nearly made me give up night fishing also. Let him who doubts try to unhook an eel among thistles by the light of the stars and a wax match. Later in the same summer, however, I came upon an ancient bream-fisher at dusk perched on a camp-stool, and brooding over the quiet waters like some sad heron. Attached to the top of his float was a feather blacker than the impending gloom, and therefore visible against the water-line longer than anything else.

A man of few words, that ancient. He may perhaps have been susceptible to the mysteries of night, the rustling and whispering of unseen creatures, the melancholy owls in the woods behind, the low murmur of the restless river, the reflected track of the stars growing ever fainter as dawn approached, to the deathly chill of the darkest hour. But of these things he said nothing; his hope was a sackful of bream before sunrise. I sometimes pick up out of a drawer a queer little black object with a fat white head, which I am informed is a 'luminous' float, and so often as I do so I think of that old bream-fisher sitting solitary through the nights, and wonder whether he ever could meet the river-god face to face. For my part, I never catch anything to speak of in the dark, and the luminous float goes back into the drawer where it has lain all these years unused.

One old writer, by the way, two hundred years ago commended to his disciples the use of glow-worms imprisoned in a clear quill float, and is minute in his instructions as to getting the best light out of them! But I suspect him of depending on tradition rather than on experience. He is more practical when he comes to a float of reed:

'Note, if at any time the angler should be destitute of floats when he comes to the water-side to angle, and there be e'er a dry sound reed to be gotten, cut it close to the joints, leaving two joints to every float uncut, one at one end, and another at t'other, to keep out the water; it will make a good float in time of need.'

Float-caps are most pleasing when cut out of quill and stained deep red, but most practical when cut from a length of fine black indiarubber tubing. A foot of this will last a season through. You can also embellish your floats yourself if you please. A long swan quill can be given a coat of Lincoln green and a head of crimson with the aid of varnish stain or enamel, and it is then sufficiently attractive to be the companion of one's days. The true test of matrimony is said to be continued ability on the part of the persons involved to survey each other across the breakfast-table without weariness. If you consider that the angler often has to watch his float, motionless 'a painted ship upon a painted ocean', for hours, with no intrinsic interest beyond the float and the watching, you will perceive that a fair appearance has its value here also. But, of course, one is best pleased with one's float as it vanishes from sight, so I will not seek to press the analogy too closely. Moreover, you can always change your float when you get tired of it, and try another with a new colour scheme. If luck counts for anything, it is sometimes worth doing. But there is a thing about floats which I have noticed sorrowfully, and cannot explain. The one which looks nicest, sits best in the water, and reveals most bites, always is to be found on the line of the other man. To comprehend this one must, I fancy, plumb deeper depths than those of angling.

CHAPTER SIXTEEN

Thoughts on Big Fish

A trout is, I take it, a big one according to circumstances. I have seen a man in one watershed with mouth open and eyes a-goggle on a fish of one pound being produced for his inspection. On another watershed I have seen the same man carefully returning a fish of over that weight to the stream with hardly a groan, or anyhow with no more complaint than is permissible to a wet fly fisher newly introduced to a chalkstream, One's memories of big ones, therefore, must necessarily be coloured by the conditions in which they were caught or seen - in my case more often seen than caught, and I think it is those that were merely seen that have left the most piquant memory behind them.

I remember once taking a country walk with a friend who is now dead. It was just a country walk with no atmosphere of fishing about it. He was no fisherman and so far as I knew there were no trout within miles. But it was lovely country and hot summer and I was quite happy. About lunch time we sought the hospitality of a cottage standing a little back from the road in a clump of trees and there procured a simple meal. It proved to be one of the lodges of some big estate, and after eating we trespassed a little, because I had seen the glint of water through the trees and I can never resist looking at water. It proved to be the narrow end of a large lake and there on its bank we sat us down to smoke and digest for a little before going on our way.

Presently we became aware of several large fish which sailed lazily in and out of a sort of weedrack or grating which crossed the water. 'What are those?' asked my friend. 'Carp,' I said promptly, for they were too big to be anything else, though they were too far off to be clearly distinguished. Presently, however, their wanderings gradually brought them nearer, and to my astonishment I perceived that if they were carp they had miraculously acquired adipose fins. Of course they were trout and they were certainly the most distinguished company for average size that I have ever seen in my life. The smallest must have been over three pounds and the biggest may well have been six or seven pounds. I suppose there were eight or ten of them in view. I have often wondered since whether they were a fair sample of the stock in that lake and speculated what, in that case, a day's fishing there would be like. They did not give the impression of being educated fish and I have always believed that the water would give a sort of record bag.

But one cannot tell. I have tried one or two lakes where trout reach a heavy old age almost undisturbed and found that the patriarchs seem to absorb wisdom without the customary course of instruction, which has been very disappointing to me. Perhaps it is as well that I have never had the chance of being disenchanted on that other water. It can remain a sort of dream fishery with a five-pound average and no reservations, mental or actual.

The biggest trout I ever saw alive and in the water was in the Kennet at Newbury, at the extreme bottom of the Piscatorial Society's stretch which is known as 'The Three Fields.' It was about 6 a.m. I had come out soon after daybreak with some idea of fishing, but had found the river too low for anything owing to the action of the mills which,

I suppose, were holding back water for their day's work. So I sat on the boundary fence and meditated on things in general and on the differing aspects of a river when it is full and when it is nearly empty. I was roused by a splashing a little below, and looking round I perceived a really enormous trout with half its back out of the water rolling about and gathering in minnows by the mouthful. It was a magnificent fish with deep golden flanks and it looked fully a yard long, perhaps more. I never dared to say what I really thought at the time as to its weight, but I have always boldly maintained that it could not have been less than fifteen pounds. That would be a modest and retiring estimate for the fish I saw. Later in the same year there was some confirmation of the existence of this monster, when an angler who had been trying for the barbel which sometimes lie in a hole a little higher up - or even, in the early weeks of the season, on the shallow itself - returned with a thrilling story of a colossal trout which had taken the worm and smashed his tackle after a furious battle. What was the fish's ultimate fate I know not. I never heard any more of it.

I have seen a few other very big trout in the Kennet, nothing to compare with that one, but fish that might be nearly ten pounds. In most years there are one or two which

live close to the water bridge right in Newbury town and I have seen a monster or so in other parts of the river.

The biggest Thames fish I ever saw was the one in Benson weirpool, a fish of possibly thirteen or fourteen pounds from the splash of him. I remember a huge trout that used to live in the Colne at Uxbridge, which looked like a ten-pounder, but it was a black fish and may not have weighed so much as its length suggested. In one or two other rivers I have seen an occasional trout which might be getting on for that weight. One of them, oddly enough, was the Great Ouse, which is as little of a trout stream as any river we possess. It was at Holywell Ferry and I was drifting quietly downstream in a boat, looking into the water for some signs of those big perch which haunt that part of the river, when my eye lighted on a great fish with spots, an undoubted trout and a big one. I believe there have always been a few trout in the reach below St. Ives, which is much of it gravelly and not very deep, and recently I have seen accounts of some being noticed in the Staunch Pit below St. Ives' lock. Perhaps they are descendants of the fish I saw.

For those who have never seen a really big trout in the water and who yearn to do so, the observation post I could best recommend from my own experience would be the great dam at Blagdon. You may not fish from the dam, but you are allowed to walk along the top of it to get to the lake shore beyond. On a bright, calm day you are very likely to see, with its chin resting on one of the sloping concrete blocks, a trout which will make your heart beat faster. On one occasion I saw two, about forty yards apart, which I am sure were fully twelve pounds apiece. One was a light fish, the other a dark one. The next evening I was in a boat and I need hardly say that I made for the dam in the hope of stirring one of the giants. Nor need I say that I might just as well have fished away at Ubley for all the response I got. You can often in calm weather reconstruct big fish at Blagdon from certain signs, the tip of a nose at one point, a back fin behind it and a tail behind that. Sometimes there are appalling distances between these objects as some veteran lazily rolls among the olive midges after sunset. But that is not the same as actually taking in the length and width of the creature at your leisure, as you can from the vantage point of the dam. Therefore I recommend that promenade for the purpose. Sometimes, of course, one sees nothing there except a three-pounder or so, but I am always disappointed if I have passed along without spotting something out of the common.

To the end of one's angling life, I suppose one will continue at times to be misled by the appearance of things, and of fish among them. Every season I get an occasional disappointment on catching some trout which, seen at a distance, had struck me as being beyond the common in point of size. But a short time ago I had a rather ignominious experience of this kind. In a tiny stream in which I had acquired angling rights, though circumstances had prevented me from making much use of them, I discovered a red trout lying at the point where the water, from being a system of two or three nothings making damp threads through a meadow, concentrates itself into a single channel and is recognisable as a brook. There is, in fact, a little pool at this point and in this pool I could see two or three trout, particularly the big red one.

He looked very impressive in so small a place, and I unhesitatingly estimated him at two and a half pounds, which would be a huge fish for the water, whose average weight is more like ten ounces. And I was confirmed in my opinion when after taking my Wickham's Fancy he bolted downstream into a clump of rushes and smashed my cast as if it had been cobweb. Worse than this, I confided my opinion to one or two others who might be interested in the matter and committed myself to the story that the brook held trout up to two and a half pounds. That sort of story gives a fishery dignity and importance.

I only had one more day's fishing there before the season closed and then I was unfortunate enough to catch, among others, my red trout, whom I found lying in exactly the same place and on whom I tried forcing tactics as soon as I had hooked him, on a Cochybonddu this time. I found the forcing tactics unexpectedly successful, the reason being clear when the fish came to the spring balance and made no more than one pound five ounces. Seldom have I been worse deceived by a fish; I suppose the confined space in which he had his abode made him seem disproportionately big. Fortunately on the same day I discovered another trout in a little hatch-hole which enabled me to stick to the 'up to two and a half pounds' account. His head and shoulders must have weighed that, though I question whether the rest of him weighed anything. He was a lamentable twenty inches of trout.

I fully expected to catch him when I saw what he was like (though as a matter of fact I did not), for the reason that if there is a decrepit fish anywhere about which only weighs half what it should, it is almost certain to come and take my fly. Possibly my fondness for fishing in odd places, backwaters, carriers, millheads and the like, lays me open to this, for bad old fish certainly tend to inhabit the quieter and less vigorous parts of a water. Even the well-known monster which lies under a bridge often turns out to be mostly head, and presumably he has some easy nook behind a buttress or in an eddy where he can avoid the exertion of constantly breasting a strong stream. You do not often catch one of these bridge trout and when you do it almost always disappoints you by not coming up to your expectations of its weight.

One of my most grievous disappointments was when I marked a great trout feeding in a portion of the Kennet and Avon canal, succeeded in getting him to take a dry Wickham and for several minutes was convinced that I had on the fish of my dry fly career. He proved indeed to be about 24 inches long when at last I got him out, but unfortunately he was one of the old breed which has become dolefully familiar to me, and instead of weighing a good seven pounds as he should have, he only touched four and a half pounds. In the water, of course, he seemed much more than that owing to his great length and as I was using fine gut the fight was long enough to have been put up by a six or seven-pounder.

As a matter of fact I have only once caught a bigger fish with dry fly and that was at Blagdon, so it could scarcely claim special honours. It was satisfactory, however, as rewarding a real bit of dry fly work. I found the fish rising late in the evening in the Butcombe Bay end (the lake was low that summer, so there was a good deal of river in evidence), covered it with a sedge just as if it had been a Kennet fish, and landed it after a real hard fight, four and three-quarter pounds. I remember the clock striking ten as I lifted it out in my landing net.

This was a fish of reasonable shape and solidity, but I remember another big Blagdon trout which was less satisfactory. This was also caught on a dry fly. It had been found rising steadily just inside a clump of weeds which was within easy casting distance of the bank. It was feeding in the very deliberate manner which is suggestive of a heavy trout and when after some time I persuaded it to take a fly - a hackle fly not unlike the Brown Silverhorns that were about in plenty - I expected something extra special in the way of a battle.

The result was surprising. The hooked fish hardly resisted at all, gave a feeble waggle or two and then allowed itself to be towed ashore. The reason for this was plain then - it was very badly deformed. Though it had the length and framework of a big one, it also had a double spinal curvature, and as might be expected, was anything but athletic and poorly nourished to boot. The surprising thing was that the fish, a rainbow, had been able, despite physical disabilities which must have attended it from the fry stage, to live and grow to a weight of nearly three pounds.

Rainbows are rather apt to be disappointing on the scales because of their short life and their tendency to deteriorate at an age when brown trout would still be putting on ounces. I caught one once at Ravensthorpe Reservoir, the lake which is famous as one of the early proofs of what results can be got from trout culture in water storage lakes, which was rising just like that Blagdon fish, with heavy deliberation suggestive of great size. And it *was* a big fish, or rather it had been once. It was shaped more like an eel than a trout and, even so, it weighed two and a half pounds. I have no doubt that in happier days it had been at least twice as heavy.

But, as I have said, it has been my luck to meet with that sort of fish very frequently, so an instance more or less no longer surprises me. I could wish that I was less favoured with regard to big ones of that type.

I do not remember ever hooking and losing the sort of

trout that makes history, or at any rate the sort of trout that I honestly believed would have made history. I am not exempt, of course, from the common fisherman's failing of estimating 'the big one that got away' on a perhaps too generous scale. The biggest trout that I ever hooked, of which I am certain, I was fortunate enough to land.

It came from the famous weirpool at Uxbridge and weighed two ounces under eight pounds. It took a dilapidated metal spinning bait of the Devon type and gave me a great fight. I had at that time never seen a trout out of the water of anything like such a size and I had no idea what it would weigh. Five pounds was as much as I dared to hope for, so my pride and joy when the scales at the keeper's cottage revealed the truth can be imagined. It was a beautiful fish 25 inches long and with deep, gleaming flanks, a picture of an old Colne trout. I had other good and handsome fish from that pool and the stream below afterwards, but nothing to approach that one. The biggest was four and a half pounds. Another angler a few years later got one of seven and a quarter pounds. The Colne has in its time yielded a good many fish of about that size, but I am afraid that some parts of it have now seen their best days. The extraordinary catches at West Drayton made during the years when the water was heavily stocked with big fish, suggest that the river may yet be capable of recovery. The fish seem to thrive well enough in its lower reaches, though of course the Thorney Weir records are not due to the natural breeding capacities of the stream.

I should not like to assert positively that I ever hooked anything bigger than the second trout on my list either. This weighed six and three-quarter pounds and was caught at Blagdon on a gold-bodied fly which has since done a good deal of execution on the lake and which Donald Carr, I believe, christened 'The Field.' It is really not much more than an elaboration of the Wickham by the addition of a topping and a red tail; but it is a very killing pattern for big trout of minnowing propensities. Such a fish on my first day at Blagdon made me very pleased with myself, especially as it was companioned in my bag by two others of four pounds ten ounces and three pounds eight ounces. Another man got one of nearly the same weight on that day and it was an extraordinary circumstance that there was not another trout over six pounds caught for some years. The eight and nine-pounders, average weights of five pounds or more, and other portents that made Blagdon so famous all belonged to the two seasons before my first visit.

Afterwards the weight of the fish caught fell considerably, though latterly it has been going up again. The big ones were still there - as I said earlier, I have seen some of them - but for some obscure reason nobody caught any for several seasons. There were tragic losses each year though, and it may have been simply luck. One reason why fish used to be lost there at first was the fact that so many men visited the lake with ordinary trout tackle, the sort of gear which would be well enough for waters where the fish run up to a pound and a half or so, but which was no good for a six-pounder which behaved like a torpedo. Gut should be strong for such a fish and there should be plenty of backing on the reel.

When I get down to lesser weights I can point proudly to considerable losses. The worst certainly was that of a trout which I hooked on a dry fly in a small tributary of the Kennet. I am sure that trout was over five pounds and he would have been the most valued of all my trophies. I had him on for a full quarter of an hour, most of which he spent in a thick clump of sedges right at my feet. He had run a good long way downstream after being hooked and then turned into the sedges and burrowed well in before I realised what he was doing.

I tried every conceivable method of getting him out and finally endeavoured to tail him - by wetting my arm almost to the shoulder I could just manage to get a hold on him. But, alas! the tail of a trout is not as that of a salmon and he slipped through my grasp, broke the gut and was gone. I can remember sitting on a gate for half an hour after that wondering, whether I should drown myself immediately or take the next train back to London, for I knew that I should never have another chance with that trout and I never did.

In earlier days there had been a hatch of mayfly on that little stream and then it was possible to look forward hopefully. There was a fish of just under four pounds which I had lost three times in one season and finally killed on a mayfly. But to find a five-pounder taking small flies on a second occasion was beyond expectation, for such fish are very incurious about small flies as a rule.

I once had a mayfly day on the Kennet which must have totalled up a large number of lost pounds. It seemed to my excited imagination that I hooked all the biggest trout in the fishery one after the other. They varied from four pounds to six pounds. I do not think there was anything over six pounds though I was quite in the vein to have lost Big Ben himself had I been able to find him. Big Ben was a local institution, said to weigh fifteen pounds but he never gladdened my eyes or subsequently filled my heart with sorrow. His smaller brethren did their best, however, and I was quite sufficiently desperate at the day's end with a paltry brace just over the limit of a pound and a half in my basket and a long list of defeats in my mind.

Sedge fishing has provided most of us with experience of trout which were presumably of unusual size, but it is not at all easy to be certain even in one's mind. I well remember a tremendous battle with a Kennet trout hooked on a sedge when it was nearly dark. That fish took me downstream for quite 300 yards and felt like a salmon the whole way. Had I lost him at the end of it I should unhesitatingly have put him down as seven pounds at least. As a matter of fact he weighed three pounds five ounces and proved to have been hooked in one of the ventral fins. For that reason I have never liked to be too positive about trout which have got off after being hooked in the late evening.

But I have twice had dealings with fish that felt as the Kennet fish and for a considerable time had me absolutely helpless to stop or turn them on their downward course. One was in the Itchen and the other in the Test and both made nothing of a powerful rod and strong gut. Both got off before I had a chance of seeing them. I have had one similar contest besides in the Itchen, but that was in daylight and I was and am pretty sure that the fish was a huge grayling; there were known to be several very big ones at the spot where it was hooked.

Except in southern waters I have had very little experience of big trout and I have never had the luck to catch anything out of the common on mountain streams or lakes when I have been definitely fishing for trout. I have had a few relatively big ones when salmon fishing. Once I got hold of one of those old stagers for which the Coquet is famous. I thought it was a grilse when it fastened at the end of a long line, but after quite a respectable fight, considering the sixteen-foot rod and salmon gut, I pulled in a big brown trout of at least four pounds. Fortunately - it was in October - he was lightly hooked and kicked himself off, so the experience cannot have done him any harm. Had I got him out I should have been tempted to weigh him and that might not have improved his health so near the spawning time.

CHAPTER SEVENTEEN

Blagdon

Life is largely composed of regrets, some bigger, some smaller. One of my very biggest is that on a certain May morning in the year 1905 I was not at Blagdon, whither I had been bidden by one of the great anglers of our time. As things were, I was gazing dolefully upon the Wye in flood - ten feet of flood there were, I remember - and wondering how Lorenzo was faring the while. And how was he faring? Five brace of trout weighing some fifty pounds - that was approximately his modest basket. Other things being equal, I would, I think, sooner fish for salmon than trout, but when the trout are such trout, when one reflects that never in the history of English fishing had there been such an opportunity as Blagdon offered that May, and when... But one cannot go into the whole appalling business and still keep calm. I might have caught an eight-pounder! Lorenzo did, then or soon afterwards. I might...

It was not till the opening day of the following season that I made first acquaintance with the wonderful Somerset lake which has inspired so many angling rhapsodies, and then I was a year too late. By that I mean a year too late for great baskets of monsters running from four pounds to eight or nine pounds. It will, I trust, never be too late for a fisherman to know and love Blagdon. It is still, and always will be, a delightful place, and though its fishing has altered in character, I am not sure that it is not even more interesting

149

now than it was of old. I cannot speak, of course, with the experience of Lorenzo and those others who reaped such a harvest in 1905, but I did just get a glimpse of the golden age on that opening day of 1906. I learnt what it was like to have a real big Blagdon trout bending the rod and filling the soul with terror; I saw the end of the old order. And since then I have watched it giving place to the new, and though for that great lost opportunity there must always be regret, I am not sure that I did not enjoy my last visit to Blagdon more than the first.

The lake, as most people know, is one of the reservoirs which supply the needs of the great city of Bristol; but though the work of men's hands, it has as much beauty as any place of Nature's making. At one end there is a great stone dam, and there is some suggestion of prose about the buildings behind it, but turn your back on them and you have nothing but poetry. On the right lies Blagdon village, scattered delightfully over twin spurs of Blackdown, a fortunate village, which seems to have grown naturally in the most becoming manner, not too crowded nor yet too widespread, a village whose very existence is an answer to those who cavil at the English nation for not being blessed with artistic sense. I have known rises from four-pounders missed because the angler was so busy admiring Blagdon village, with its grey church tower and wealth of fruit blossom, and one cannot praise it more highly than by that confession.

On the left lie richly wooded slopes with a picturesque farm or two nestling among the trees. In front is the lake almost as far as one can see, perhaps three-quarters of a mile wide at the Blagdon end, and gradually narrowing till one comes to the mouth of the River Yeo, which runs in past Ubley Mill, grey stone among the trees, where are the stock-ponds and hatchery. All round the lake are hills, Blackdown, the highest point of the Mendips, being one of them. Its thousand-odd feet show very impressively when thunder threatens, and afford a superb spectacle when the lightning plays upon their summit. To agitated human beings at that time the ascent to the village and shelter is formidable. I shall never forget the race that Lorenzo and I raced one Sunday afternoon, or the breathlessness of our entry just before the deluge.

The lake itself is more than commonly attractive. It is no mere ordinary sheet of water with a deep portion in the middle, shallow portions at the sides, and the other features of 'expectedness,' if I may so term it. A chart showing all the variations and inequalities in its depth and bottom would be an interesting but complicated thing. Winding tortuously through the middle of the lake is the old river-bed of the Yeo, and crisscrossed everywhere are ditches, dykes, a submerged lane or so, with occasional little pools and pot-holes marking the spots once occupied by duck-ponds or depressions in the fields. One result of this is that anywhere one is likely to come upon an unexpected bit of deep water subtly disposed even in a shallow corner, and of course, in such a place one expects to find a big trout lurking secure, but willing, if one can but put a fly before him. Another result is that the bank angler is tempted to take plenty of exercise, for beyond every bend he hopes for some of that variety which is so calculated to lure him on. There is something particularly tempting about the Blagdon ditches, dark blue or olive ribbons stretching out across the yellow or brown of the shallows.

On my first visit the lake was quite full, and its circumference was a mighty thing - some seven miles, I should say, taking all the bays and corners into consideration. Part of the distance is heavy and moist going (knee-boots or wading-stockings are a wise precaution), and the man who desires to fish all round it in the day needs good legs and a 'merry heart'. A few energetic souls make the round without apparently regarding it as a matter for pride. One or two, whose hearts can hardly be able to contain their merriness if Shakespeare is right, do it before breakfast, and turn up smiling about 5 p.m., having done it again. But the ordinary out-of-condition mortal will find one circuit in the course of the day as much as prudence dictates, while the cautious one will only attempt to cover so much ground as can be done without undue fatigue and with due regard to return.

This last point is worth bearing in mind, for when one is half-way round, the distance covered is no wise less in returning the way one came than in completing the circle. I was all for a cautious procedure, but consuming curiosity as to what lay beyond every next promontory led me on and on until the thing was done, and backward steps were become, if not impossible, at least ineffectual.

The flies commonly used for Blagdon trout are smallish salmon flies - Silver Doctor, Jock Scott, Silver Grey, and the like. March Brown and Alexandra take their toll of the fish, and there is a fly with a gold body which has been dubbed 'The Field' by Donald Carr, the head-ranger. I introduced it at my first visit, and it killed well for a couple of seasons, but I fancy it has pretty well exhausted its magic by now. It is little more than Wickham with a red tail and one or two extra adornments. Salmon flies require something powerful in the way of a rod, and I started with a fourteen-foot split cane, which I did not find a bit too big for bank-fishing. Even for boat work I believe a double-handed rod would have advantages, as the trout often rise within a yard or two of the boat, and a single-handed rod sometimes fails to drive the big hook home. But conditions now are not quite what they were, as I hope to show later.

On the first day I fished Blagdon conditions were unfavourable, the wind being cold and the fish sulky. There had, it subsequently appeared, been misfortunes among the sticklebacks. Either they had all been eaten or had died some other way; at any rate, there were none visible, and so the big trout were not close in shore chasing them, or lying in wait as they ought to have been. The stock of sticklebacks has since been renewed, with great advantage to the bank-fisher, but that day I flogged sturdily on for a mile or more, and saw nothing except the spectacle of a friend's rod bending in the distance - bending to no purpose, because the fish got off after a bit of a fight.

For another hour there was no further sign of Blagdon fish, but I persevered along the north shore, casting across a strong north-westerly wind. I then decided on a change of fly, discarded the dropper, a Silver Doctor, and replaced the March Brown at point with one of the 'Field' flies already mentioned. This soon aroused the curiosity of a fish, but he merely followed it and did not take. My first real rise was got in a bay where a deep channel about four feet wide ran out into the lake, showing dark amid the shallower water. Fishing across the bay, dropping the fly just on the far side of this channel and working it towards me, I got five rises in about as many yards of water and in quick succession. But though three of them seemed to mean business, nothing came of it. One fish ran a few yards and was off, another jumped and was off, and the third was off after holding the fly for a second. All three seemed fish of four pounds or thereabouts.

The series of misfortunes was disappointing, but I consoled myself by thinking that the trout had evidently now begun to feed, and that it would only be a matter of minutes before the first fish was in the bag. But never a rise did I get during the next hour and a half, nor did I see another fish move, and by the time I joined my friend a mile farther on for lunch, I was of the opinion that the Blagdon trout were lunching light that day. My friend, I found, had not stirred a fish since his loss, and two other anglers who passed by had not killed anything either. Altogether, the prospects looked bad.

After lunch my friend decided to retrace his steps, and I went on to explore, as we were fully half-way round. The edge of the lake in this part was rather shallow, but here and there were narrow channels of the kind described, which certainly looked as if they should yield something. It was not, however, till I came to the point where the lake gets a good deal narrower that I saw a sign of another fish. Here there was a regular dyke running out from the shore; it looked as if it might originally have been a road. To fish it one had to cast right into the wind, and the fly fell with more force than precision. At the mouth, however, and in about five feet of water, a fish came at my gold-bodied fly like a tiger and went off well hooked. From its play I thought at first that it must be a big rainbow. It came out of the water several times and fought desperately for the open lake. The gut, however, was suited to the rod and fly, and the fish never got out more than ten yards of line at a burst, eventually coming into the big net dead-beat.

On the shore it proved to be a brown trout, bright in colour, though rather long in proportion to its girth. The spring balance made it about four and half pounds. I was now well satisfied, having got a Blagdon trout in spite of sticklebacks and other disadvantages, and having saved what looked like being a blank.

From the scene of triumph to the end of the lake the water within reach of the rod seemed shallow, and the wind made casting difficult, so I made my way on to the corner where the channel of the River Yeo runs in. There is a short stretch of the river itself between the road and the lake which can be fished. It is only about twenty feet broad in most places, but it is deep, and sometimes yields a good fish. Standing well back from the bank, I began to cast about half-way down with a short line.

The fly had not travelled a yard before there was a great boil, and I was into something that raced away upstream like a salmon. It kept deep, and I got no sight of it for some time, until it turned and came back at the same pace for its starting-point, and then jumped. After that it tried to bore right under my own bank, but the long rod was fortunately able to check that proceeding, and the rest of the fight was carried on in the depths. It must have been nearly ten minutes before I finally got the trout into the net and carried it, exulting, back into the meadow. It was just like playing a small salmon, and I can well believe that the fish would have run out fifty or sixty yards of line, as Blagdon trout sometimes do, if it had been hooked on the shallows in the open lake. It was a shapely, silvery fish, and I tried to persuade myself that my spring balance and I were in accord in regarding it as seven pounds.

The too truthful scales at the hut, however, would not compromise with us in the evening, and it was only six and three-quarter pounds then. A cup of tea and a brief rest could, now that the brace was assured, be enjoyed with a quiet conscience. Afterwards, I fished the river down again, caught a third trout of three pounds ten ounces, and rose two others, one of them evidently a big one.

There is an element of irony as well as luck about my first catch at Blagdon. With my mind full of possible seven and eight pounders, it never occurred to me that I ought to have the big one put into a glass case, cast, modelled, or otherwise made immortal, albeit much the biggest I have ever caught on a fly. In the previous year a fish of six and three-quarter pounds would have been nothing out of the way. But - there has not been a trout so big caught at Blagdon since! A fish of six pounds six ounces was killed by a boat angler on the same day, and I think one or two others may have been taken later which just exceeded six pounds, but I am pretty certain there have not been half a dozen of them in the four seasons that have elapsed since the great year 1905. I wish I had realized how lucky I was, and done the right thing by my trophy, instead of letting it be ingloriously eaten. Not even a paper outline remains to tell the tale.

After that first day, luck seemed to desert me at Blagdon. I fished it from boat, I fished it from bank, and caught hardly anything. In fact, I began to regard the place as bewitched, so blank were my days, so vile the weather. Each subsequent visit seemed to give less result than the one before it, though other anglers continued from time to time to get their six or eight fish, averaging about three pounds. I suspect that Fate thought I had had as much success as was good for me, and set herself to humble my proud spirit. She did it. I well remember one of the days she gave me.

It was about the worst Blagdon has ever known. The wind from the north-west was bitterly cold, and about luncheon-time the waves at the upper end of the lake were running mountains high and foam-crested. Carr's manful work with the sculls and my diligent casting with the flies resulted in exactly one short rise. All we could do was to hope for a cessation of wind and a warmer time towards evening. Meanwhile, I left the boat and tried casting a small fly-spoon from the shore. Result - one two-year-old returned, and one better fish hooked and lost. After that tea in the fishing-hut, and then to ship again. The wind really did begin to drop about 5 p.m. and I began to hope once more; but a long, long drift yielded not so much as a rise, and we exchanged gloomy views as to the weight of the bag.

Then all of a sudden the trout began to show themselves, practically for the first time in four days. All round the boat great fish were coming up with a quiet swirl or roll, some of them showing head and shoulders, others only a broad tail. It was really a wonderful sight for the three-quarters of an hour it lasted, and I felt quite certain that I was going to make up for lost time. I worked tremendously hard, got wonderfully excited, tried fly after fly, great and small - moderately small, that is - covered fish after fish, and caught nothing. I never saw so many big fish moving in my life as on that evening, but I touched not a single one of them. It was tantalization of the worst kind. I then and there registered a vow never to go near Blagdon again.

Of course one does not keep that sort of vow, and I have since in a very modest way had improved sport, but by an alteration of method. The sight of those big fish that evening, all of them apparently feeding on surface food - there was a good deal of fly on the water - caused me to meditate deeply, and I finally came to the conclusion that I ought to have tried them with quite small flies, not merely the loch patterns which had been used as a change, but real imitations of the insects on and in the water. Opportunity for testing this theory properly did not come for some time (I had some small results on one visit), but at last, in September, 1909, I found myself at Blagdon once more in company with M., a very cunning fisher, who ties his own flies, and can imitate anything on the spur of the moment. We were both resolute to give the small fly, especially the dry fly, a trial, and see whether something could not be done with it.

Thundery skies, tearing winds, and driving rain - the mixed weather of our visit - were much against us, though they were not so hostile to the ordinary and perhaps more productive kind of fishing. Still, we had some results, such as they were. M., who set about the business in the most resourceful manner, had better results than I. The joint bag of three days confirms me in the opinion that in some circumstances it would pay anglers to use small flies even for Blagdon's big fish.

This is not a new doctrine, of course. I know that many good fishermen have used, and do use, the small fly there from time to time with more or less success. But I am inclined to think that either conditions or the trout's habits have changed somewhat, and that small flies are now better worth a trial than ever they were before. That they can supersede the salmon-fly altogether I do not believe, but they may certainly serve as a valuable addition to it. The fish, big ones as well as small, undoubtedly feed at some times either on fly, fly larvae, or other small food, and when they are doing that they are to be caught with an imitation of the natural insect. When, on the other hand, they are feeding on sticklebacks, the salmon-fly is obviously a better lure, as it is when they are not visibly feeding at all, and have to be fetched up from the bottom.

The small fly, therefore, according to our experience, is the thing to use when there is a rise, the big fly at most other times. On some days, it may be, there will not be a rise at all, for that depends on the amount of fly on the water; but ever then, a certain number of fish may possibly be found in very shallow water, cruising about with their back fins or tails showing from time to time. If there is no fly about, such fish are probably taking the little beetles of the water-boatman type, which simply swarm all over the lake, or hunting for sticklebacks; an occasional rush and boil will show when these are the quarry. Sometimes, at any rate, a feeder of this sort will take a dry fly.

After a dull morning, during which I had flogged away with two grilse flies all along the shore, from the embankment to the corner where Butcombe stream runs in, I at last found a fish cruising on the shallows at the edge of the river. Once, at least, he made a rush eloquent of sticklebacks, but took no notice of the silver-bodied fly which fell near him. However, he still continued to feed. I changed the tackle, tied on a Wickham on a No. 3 hook, and put it over him, or rather near him, dry. He literally rushed upon it from quite two yards away, and after a longish fight I got him out, a brown trout of three pounds, rather lanky, but otherwise in good condition.

After that I had an interview with a wasp, a sleepily vicious September brute, which was anxious to make someone pay for the wet day that was annoying it, and which - I grieve to have to confess it - put me to head-long flight. Worse than that, it followed doggedly in pursuit, until there was nothing for it but to turn and give battle. It settled on me two or three times, hat and glasses fell off, and altogether it was an anxious time. I won in the end, but the moral victory was with my assailant. I have never been at my ease with wasps since I stirred up a nest with the handle of my landing-net, inadvertently, of course.

To return to the fishing, a little later I met M., and found that he had got a noble brace, one a rainbow of three and a half pounds, and the other a brown trout of three three-quarter pounds, both on dry fly, a hackle sedge of his own tying, besides a small rainbow of one and a quarter pounds, which he had kept for breakfast - and choicely good it was at that meal. He had been using only a little nine-foot split cane, and had had a rare fight with each of the big ones. We had an early tea, and got on the water again about 4 p.m. I stayed on the Blagdon shore near the embankment, and he went along towards Butcombe.

The sky cleared by five o'clock, a gleam of sun heralded a fine evening, and opposite to where I was, fish began to rise or bulge. There were eight or ten of them within reach of a long cast, but they wandered a great deal, and the wind in my face was troublesome. I am not sure that I covered more than two of them fairly. Of these I caught one, two and three-quarter pounds, and rose the other, both with the Wickham fished dry. The second took me unawares as I was lighting a cigarette, the fly meanwhile resting placidly on the water, and the first intimation I had of it was seeing the line drawn out.

Of course I missed him. The rest either did not see my fly, or, probably, would have none of it, but it was a fascinating business, as some of them were undoubtedly very big fish; the distance between their heads and tails seemed very spacious. It was purely a local rise, for when M. turned up at dusk he reported that he had scarcely seen a fish move. The bank-fisher at Blagdon must, I think, expect to find the rise generally rather local. The sheltered shore is usually the best to make for, but this evening it was not so.

The morrow was Sunday, and of course a perfect

day, and fish were rising well, some of them close inshore. Monday, when we resumed the rod, was horrid, a day of gloom and occasional rain. M. got a brace of rainbows in the morning (best, two pounds two ounces), both on a small green-bodied fly that he had tied to imitate a gnat which the fish were taking on Saturday, and which he fished wet. I got nothing till the evening, when I found three or four rainbows rising in a sheltered bay, rose three of them with a Greenwell's Glory, No. 3 hook, sparsely dressed, fished wet, but only landed one, one and three-quarter pounds. About 6.30 p.m. what rise there was stopped altogether, and M. went home. I put on a tiny Silver Doctor, the smallest I possessed, and followed him slowly, keeping a lookout for minnowing fish.

Two such were discovered. One, a rainbow of about two pounds, was lost after a longish fight. The other took me at the entrance to a ditch, and went off like a mad thing, running out thirty or forty yards of line in two rushes, and making me tremble for the gut, which was rather fine. But I got him at last, a big brown trout which weighed about an ounce less than four pounds, and should have been considerably more. The fly was certainly a salmon-fly, but it was several sizes smaller than any salmon-fly I had used at Blagdon before, so I was pleased.

Tuesday was certainly not 'my day out.' I saw never a rise before 6 p.m. and then, just as the fun was beginning, the cold wind, strong all day, but apparently dropping, freshened once more and all was up with my chances on the Blagdon shore. I got one brown trout of two and a half pounds with a Silver Doctor, No. 9 and that was all. M., on the other hand, was very successful, for he returned from the far and sheltered shore with two trout, one a rainbow of about one and three-quarter pounds, the other a really big brown trout of five and a quarter pounds. This, I believe, was the heaviest fish caught at Blagdon that year and he got it on a dry Wickham and with his little nine foot rod. He would probably have caught others, for they were rising well, but had spent most of the evening over a monster which was feeding steadily, but would not take anything he could offer it.

On this subject of small flies and Blagdon trout, it may be interesting to state what those caught had been feeding on. In one we found some snails, in two or three a stickleback or so; but the bulk of the food consisted of the large green-bodied gnats already mentioned, which were round the lake in myriads on some days, and at times pretty thick on the water, of green larvae, which were presumably the nymphs of the said gnats, of the little beetles mentioned before, and of a fly which I took to be a silverhorn. This fly is very plentiful, and lasts most of the summer. The green gnat would be fairly well imitated by grass-green body, sparse but long, white hackle, and whitish hackle-point wings. The other would be more difficult, but a lightly dressed March Brown would not be a bad rendering, and a grannom might be better still, since the female carries a green egg-sac like the grannom. A No 2 hook should be small enough for either fly. We also saw a few black gnats and ants on the water, but no great quantity of either, and a good many daddy-long-legs, which are no doubt taken freely by the fish.

Doubtless on most days an angler would catch three fish in a boat for one that he would get on the bank, and probably the salmon-flies would persuade more fish than would small patterns. But it costs twice as much to fish from a boat, and one can have very excellent fun from the bank, more especially in favourable weather. On a really good day

I am sure one could have thrilling sport with the dry fly, and it is quite on the cards that one might get into one of the real monsters; there are plenty left, though they have not been caught lately. I fancy they are fairly well informed on the subject of salmon-flies, which probably accounts for it. They would not be so suspicious of small flies on finer gut. An ordinary dry-fly rod of from ten to eleven feet, a reel holding at least eighty yards of line, including backing, a good big landing-net and sound Mayfly gut are the apparatus for the work. One can reach many fish from the shore when they are on the feed, so very long casting is not needed.

For rough weather and big flies early in the season, I would still advise a double-handed rod; one could take both rods and be armed against any contingency. But my later experience shows me that by far the most enjoyable sport is to be obtained with the lighter equipment; it makes a three-pound fish as worthy a foe as was a six-pounder of old, and it makes Blagdon as desirable as ever.

CHAPTER EIGHTEEN

Some Kennet Days

Of all the south-country streams which I have fished I think my warmest affections are given to the Kennet. This is not so much on account of the sport which it has given me as of the sport which it might some day yield. The Kennet in the first week of June holds one almost breathless with exciting promises, and its trout, in the lower parts, are surely the largest offered for capture by any river that gives the flyfisher a chance. As yet no Kennet monster has come my way, but the fact that I know by sight several fish verging on ten pounds is enough to keep me expectant every succeeding Mayfly season. To me also it is an attraction that the river is not purely a trout water. Grayling, chub, dace, roach, perch and pike, all have their fascination, especially when one knows that all run big. I should say that the collector of 'specimens' would have a better chance of getting trophies from the Kennet than from any river, except, perhaps, the Hampshire Avon. But he would need patience and luck as well as skill. It is not on every day that the fish can be got to feed.

I have fished the river for a good many years now without often getting any sport worth mentioning, but I have had occasional days to be marked with a white stone. Three of them in particular, all enjoyed on the same fishery, which lies midway between Hungerford and Newbury, have induced deep gratitude in a mind not unduly spoilt by good fortune.

The first came opportunely after very trying times - times of - but no! This chapter is triumphant.

It was a windy, sunny day in August when I reached the little cart bridge which spans the water in the middle of the fishery. My mind was set on dace - fish for which this part of the Kennet is famous - and a fly-rod was in my hand. Ambition held me in its clutches; a dace weighing a pound or more was its object. Such dace in most rivers are inconceivable, but here they were a possibility; they had been caught in the past, so why should they not also brighten the future? Besides dace, there were grayling to be thought of, and it was, indeed, grayling which insisted on notice first.

Above the bridge is a shallow, a perfectly clear stretch of gravel, on which almost every fish is visible thirty yards away or more. The three big trout which occasionally come out from under the bridge and cruise round were not there, but one long dark shape in the middle of the river twenty-five yards off attracted attention. At first I thought it might be one of the three, but after making out several other rather smaller shapes near it, I came to the conclusion that it must be a grayling, and a big one. Having waders on, I decided to get in behind the shoal and attack them with a short line. The water was deeper than it looked, and when I got to within about four yards of the fish it was nearly up to the top of the waders. This, however, was an advantage in one respect: the grayling took no alarm at my proximity, and I was able to watch their every movement, except when the violent upstream wind ruffled the water too much. There were about a dozen in the shoal, ranging from some three-quarters of a pound up to the big one, who looked a good two and a half pounds.

I began the attack with a 00 double-hooked Wickham. The big one tilted his head at it once, and none of the others

would look at it. Then it was changed for a little fly with red quill body and badger hackle, also on double hooks. The patriarch came right up to inspect this, as did two or three others; but all shook their heads and tails and went down again. After several casts I tried letting the fly sink and float down under water. I could not see it now, but I could see the fish coming up to look at it just in the same way. At last it seemed to me that one of them opened his mouth and shut it again. I tightened; the grayling turned in the water and was on. Playing him gently downstream, I retreated backwards, and eventually got him into the net and to the bank without disturbing the others - a pounder with a beautiful sheen of salmon pink over his silver. After he had been placed in the creel on a bed of grass the attack was resumed. But the little fly had lost its attractions, and was changed for a Brunton's Fancy on a 00 single hook. This brought the big grayling up like a shot, and I made sure that he meant to have it. But no: down he went again, after a perceptible moment of indecision. At the next cast he did have it fairly, but somehow the strike missed him, and he went down again unpricked.

The other grayling would not take it, though several of them came and inspected it. Then I suffered it to sink and tried it under water. Again the big fish took it, and again I missed him. With another I had better luck, and after a brisk fight got him to the bank - one pound six ounces. But I could not get a third, though the fish, one or other of them, would inspect the fly every time it came down. Also the wind got worse, and it was more difficult to see what was going on. At last I gave it up and went down to the shallow below the bridge, where I knew another shoal had its home. Here the wind was very bad, and I could not see the fish at all, though an occasional rise showed me where they were. Fished dry, Brunton's Fancy produced three short rises, and fished wet accidentally one fish. I can take no credit for him, as I found he was on when I attempted to recover the line. Though he was no bigger than the first, he gave a splendid fight, and was netted with difficulty as the fly came away.

After this the wind got worse and worse, and I gave up grayling fishing as a bad job. A worm used on Stewart tackle in a hole at the bottom of the fishery on the chance of a perch would be less of a tax on the temper, and scarcely less remunerative than the dry fly. So after lunch I sat waiting for the perch to begin for pretty well three hours. One bite only rewarded my patience, and a gleam of silver as the light fly-rod bent to strike showed that the biter was no perch. It proved to be a beautiful dace, which brought the spring balance fairly down to the one-pound mark.

At last, as no more bites came, and as the wind was decreasing a little, I put on the fly-cast again, and began to fish under the other bank, where I had seen an occasional ring. It proved that there was a shoal of dace there, and for nearly an hour I wasted excellent opportunities. The wind was still gusty and unpleasant, blowing right in my teeth, and three casts out of four were futile. The fourth usually got a rise, and I usually missed the fish, or pricked and lost him. I finished about 6 p.m. with six dace, running from ten ounces to thirteen ounces, whereas I ought to have had at least twice as many.

There still remained one more incident of the day, and that the most important. I was strolling homewards, thinking all was over, as it had turned very cold, when I saw a rise on a shallow outside some rushes. I cast idly at it, and hooked the fish. Imagining that it must be a little one, I essayed to haul it ashore. But it would not be hauled, and went off downstream. Then it rolled, and I saw its depth of silver. With a gasp, I changed my tactics and played it with the most anxious care. I confess that I did not deserve the fortune, but the fish was safely landed - a noble dace of one pound two and a half ounces. I do not expect ever to get one bigger, and I am thankful to say that with the other pounder, he reached the taxidermist safely. Together in a glass case they now remain a memorial of a glorious occasion.

The next day may just be mentioned as a curiosity. The fishing was a brief affair, or rather the sport was. I reached the water about 10 a.m. By twenty minutes past I had landed the big grayling and two of his brothers, and, except for three or four little dace, I did not get another fish all day. The big grayling seriously disappointed me when I got him on to the spring balance, as he just failed to touch the two-pound mark. But in the water he was all that fancy painted.

On 5X gut and a lissome six-ounce rod he gave magnificent sport, and it must have been nearly five minutes before he was in the net, There was one moment of the combat - when he was within two yards of the bridge, and I was holding at all risks - in which I credited him with three pounds. To me grayling always look bigger in the water than they are, whereas trout generally seem smaller. But I was glad to get him, though he was below the estimate. He took, as did the others, Brunton's Fancy fished wet in the manner described. There is no better way of using it, where one can get behind one's fish and watch them. Unless the fish is in sight, a rise under water in sluggish streams is very difficult to detect. One can seldom feel it as one can in a quick stream. When the line is seen to stop it is usually too late to strike.

The second white-stone day I owe to my good friend Hyandry. The story which he related to me was frankly incredible, and I told him so. He had, he asserted, visited the fishery on Easter Monday, and had the remarkable experience of finding the big Kennet trout rising whole-heartedly at small flies, olives and trifles of that sort. He hooked, he said, no less than four of the real old stagers, besides the smaller fry of about a pound, which do not really count as Kennet fish. I knew all about those trout, for in the year when I got the big dace I fished for them assiduously, and convinced myself that, except during the Mayfly season, the big ones would rise at nothing whatsoever, unless it might be at great sedges in the twilight of the long summer evenings. Even while the Mayfly was on my efforts among the monsters were conspicuously unsuccessful - a fish of about two and a half pounds was the biggest I was able to secure. I had, indeed, seen fish heavier but they mostly stood on their heads and waved their tails in the air, supremely indifferent to surface food and dry fly anglers alike. My season on the fishery made me profoundly sceptical as to its uses as a dry fly water, except during the first half of June. Therefore, when Hyandry told tales of three-pounders feeding steadily on olives in April, I said that I should much like to see those marvels for myself - or, in other words, that he lied.

He had, moreover, had reverses, a circumstance which often stimulates incredulity. One monster, for example, ran with super-piscine swiftness downstream, doubled, jumped, and got off; another reversed these tactics, making upstream to begin with, but it looked like a five-pounder, and got off. The fourth - and here we come to the curious part of the story - did not get off. It was played with consummate skill (Hyandry knows his business; has he not captured vast sea trout with the dry fly?), landed and brought home in triumph. It weighed two pounds fourteen ounces, and was seen by credible persons. This fact certainly lent some colour to my friend's assertions. There, he could demonstrate with calm simplicity, was the fish.

On second thoughts, I had to retract what I had said about not believing him, and to admit that what he said had happened had in effect happened. But, I urged, he had stumbled on that unique occasion which is called 'once in a blue moon'. Never, never would he come upon the like again. Hyandry admitted this might be so, did not profess to explain the phenomena, and thereafter kept silence. But though silent, he was not idle, and to his good offices I attribute an invitation which reached me for a day on the water during the next week-end, a day in which I might be able to see whether Bank Holiday had been exceptional or not, and to find out whether the big trout in that part of the Kennet do take small fly in April otherwise than once in a blue moon.

I could not have had a pleasanter day for the investigation - warm, with a soft westerly breeze just strong enough to help in a long cast, and with an April shower or so to suit the season. The water, when at about 9 a.m. I stood on the well-remembered wooden bridge gazing down the long, bright shallow, looked clear and delightful, while the birds, for which the estate is famous, sang lustily, as on such a day they should. Altogether it was vastly satisfactory to be abroad whether the big trout rose or whether they did not, and I blessed my friend for procuring the chance for me. Then I saw a fly, a medium olive, and soon afterwards I became aware of rises some little way downstream, also of commotions. Hurrying down to look, I found that the rises were due to several small trout, the commotions to big grayling, which had evidently just spawned or were about to spawn. No trout of consequence, so far as I could see, was on the move, but the hatch of fly was only just beginning. In any case, I was not minded to stay by the shallow, but to go down to the bottom of the water to a favourite spot of mine of old, where I had been much tantalized by the sight of big trout, generally tailing, sometimes minnowing, but never rising, even in the Mayfly time. For some reason very few Mayflies hatched at this point - never enough to make the trout rise - though higher up the hatch might be very great.

I covered the half mile quickly, but not too soon, for the hatch was in full swing when I got to the weed-rack, which is almost at the bottom of the water. And not only was fly coming down - fish were coming up under the camp-sheathing opposite. One in particular attracted my eye, and as I watched it I mentally grovelled before Hyandry. What he had said was absolutely true, and here were the big Kennet fish doing it again; it was not even a case of a blue moon. I then became excited and nervous. I am not accustomed to seeing big fish feeding like that in

April. Moreover, the place was the last but one in the world which one would choose for an encounter with anything over a pound on such tackle as one employs for small dry flies.

The river is about twenty yards broad. The weed-rack, a pretty solid structure of piles and wire, known as the 'Stop', is shaped like a wedge, with its point upstream and in the middle of the river, and so its sides slope away to the banks, forming acute angles with the camp-sheathing. A fish hooked anywhere near the rack is morally certain to run down into the angle, and there to destroy the tackle at leisure. In fact, I discovered that such a misfortune had happened to an angler the day before, and that he had lost both fly and trout. Conscious of the difficulties of the place, but more conscious of the trout feeding, I began excitedly. He was rising only a little above the point of the weed-rack, and I had to cast slightly downstream to cover him without drag.

The first fly was a medium Olive Quill on a 00 hook, and he bulged at it twice. Then he took it, and horror! I felt that he was pricked and missed, entirely by my own fault, for I struck too soon. I could have kicked myself, and was abusing my folly, when up he came again as eager as ever. A change of fly might still save the situation. This time it was a Medium Olive Dun on a 0 hook, and he took it fair and square the first time it came over him. I now realized to the full the nature of the place, for he went irresistibly downstream, while I hurried up to get the line clear of the posts. Between us we made the reel scream, and I was sure that I should never see the fish any closer. But mercifully a memory came to me of previous fights in which guile had triumphed over force. Instead of trying to hold the fish, I slackened pressure until the line was no more than a light rein on him, and he stopped within a foot of the lowest post, and began to think it over.

It took a longish time, but foot by foot he was coaxed upstream until he was clear of the weed-rack altogether, and was swimming meditatively about in front of me. Then something - perhaps the sight of the net, which I was getting ready - started him off again, and he once more went helter-skelter for the weed-rack, this time in the angle at my own side. Here matters were complicated by a wire stretched across from the bank to the post in the middle of the river. This prevented my following, so the fight was all to begin over again. A repetition of the coaxing tactics was ultimately successful, and in the end he came into the net and was mine own. The spring balance made him out three and a half pounds - a long, thin fish, which ought to have weighed quite four pounds. But I was not disposed to be critical. A fish of that size had not often come my way to the dry fly - in April never.

Two other trout fed within a few yards of where the first was hooked. One rose, was missed, and went down. The other was in a quite inaccessible place in the farthest corner of the angle, the one spot in the world worse than that of my fight. To reach it one had to cast over the side of the weed-rack, with the certain knowledge that breaking was inevitable if the fish was hooked. I left a fly in the weed-rack and gave it up, yielding the fish to a brother angler who had just arrived.

I thought mine had been a pretty good fight, but it pales into significance beside the one he had afterwards. For, casting over the piles and wire, he hooked the trout. It ran upstream for a wonder, and he had hopes. But his line caught on one of the posts, and he could not get it clear. After waiting some time, with the fish tugging away thirty yards upstream, he decided on a desperate remedy. Twenty-five yards below the weed-rack is a railway-bridge. Paying off line, he retreated to the bridge, climbed up on to it, and, getting a straight pull, freed his line. And then the fish, now some seventy yards above him, and still going strong, gave a plunge, and the fly came away. It was a mighty contest, and about the last event of the day, for the hatch of fly was over by eleven, and the big fish all retired. But Hyandry was right. Personally, I am very glad of it.

The third great day was vouchedsafed to me in the following August, when I was again privileged to visit the water. It was very hot - so hot that I found myself wishing for coolness so early as eight o'clock. I had been out since before six, curious to see whether there would in real summer be an early morning rise. There was not, and clearly there would be none till the late evening, when the sedges come out.

On the way back to breakfast I threw out a suggestion to the keeper about worms and perch at the Stop. The Stop is the rather complicated affair for catching weeds described earlier, and is built of wire and piles. Round about it is the deepest water in the fishery, and round about it too were, I had been told, perch and - this I knew from ocular proof - roach. My notion was to sit there as on previous occasions, unsuccessful of course, but placid and relatively cool. The keeper was doubtful about the perch, but optimistic about worms. No; no gentleman had left any behind for the public good, but he dared say he could find some himself. Thereupon I went in to breakfast, reflecting that, with the worms that he would dig, the bread that should be levied from the table, and the caddises that I would collect from a ditch, the bait problem was solved. For the tackle I had my light ten-foot fly-rod, reel and gut, and friend C., who has more gear of all kinds than anyone else on earth, would surely lend me hooks and lead. This he did, and I started out again after breakfast possessed of three roach-hooks and some lead wire.

It is a longish tramp to the Stop, especially if one goes by way of the ditch, and when I got there I was both heated and caddis-less. Not one caddis had I been able to find, so all was up with the roach-fishing. Though I had duly acquired bread, I knew from experience that the roach in that water will not take it at all in August, probably from unfamiliarity with it. A course of ground-baiting might educate them. There remained, therefore, but the worms and perch. Presently, after manoeuvring the punt, providentially left there by the weed-cutters, to the position I wanted, I rigged up the tackle, a cast tapering to 3X, with a bit of lead wire wrapped round it, and one of the roach-hooks at the end. And then I opened the worm-tin.

There is room for a treatise on angle-worms, as the Americans call them, and one of its chapters should be entitled 'Worms and the Lay Mind.' The angler asks for worms. The word 'worms' has to him a special significance. It implies good measure, brimming over, a supply large enough to serve the hook all day, and to meet besides the necessities of occasional moderate ground-baiting, just to keep the fish alert. The lay mind, on the other hand, interprets it to mean three worms and a large white grub, thrown in with the idea that 'any old thing' is, piscatorially considered, a worm. I found my tin slightly better furnished - three small lobs, five assorted worms of the smallest size, and one fragment - but the supply was little enough for a morning's fishing, supposing the perch to be there and in the mood.

For a time it looked as though even this meagre stock would be too much. The Stop, as has been said, has two arms forming a wedge upstream; the punt, tied to the top post, lay along the right arm, and I fished over the posts in the V on the downstream side. The worm lay on the bottom, in about six feet of water. Nothing happened, so after a time I began to draw it about and fish all the clear water within reach - not very much, because the weeds were thick below - in the sink-and-draw fashion attractive to perch. Still nothing happened, but at last there came a striped shadow just as I was about to lift the worm out. I checked my hand, he had it at once, and was presently lost to sight and burrowing among the posts and driftweed apparently right under the punt. A steady strain brought him out, but he bolted back two or three times before the net could come into action. At last it got him, however, an honest pounder, and the worm, blown up the gut, was still intact.

After another spell of inaction, I dropped the worm in upstream of the Stop beyond the other arm, so that the rod-point projected over both rows of posts. Some care had to be exercised that the strongish current might not sweep the hook into the posts and cause disaster. Soon I felt a slow, dragging sort of bite, struck, and was battling with another fish with a similar taste for weeds and posts. It was some minutes before I even saw it, and all I could do was to hold on. The lissome fly-rod helped as it played to the fish's movements, and so saved the light gut from a smash. At last the fish was coaxed away from the piles, worked upstream, and eventually netted - a roach of one and a half pounds, which proved to be hooked in a fin and not in the mouth. Soon afterwards in the same place something else was hooked which at once bolted through the far arm of the Stop between two posts and under the wire, and plunged into the near arm at my feet, where it remained immovable.. I could do nothing but hang on and trust to luck, since the wire was between me and the rod-point and the line beneath it. At last the fish yielded to the strain and came out, now visible as a fine perch, and not a trout, as I had at first feared. Executing a strategic movement with the net, I got him just as he was meditating a turn round one of the posts - one and a half pounds.

The fine gut was now frayed pretty well to tatters, so I put on a rather stronger cast, stripping a fly to serve as hook, and tried forcible restraint with the next fish. The light seven-ounce rod was bent nearly double, but the perch never got into danger, and was netted - another pounder. Then came a fourth, a little heavier, and afterwards I hooked a bigger one. It followed the instant strain quietly enough till it was clear of the obstructions, but then it realized its situation, and dashed down on my side of the Stop and under the punt, dragging the rod-point deep into the water. I have seldom had such a fight, even with a trout, and more than once I feared for the rod. It was a relief when at last the meshes of the net received what I felt sure was a two and a half pounder. As a matter of fact, it was just short of two pounds. This fish had exhausted the last of the worms, so perch fishing seemed at an end. But a peep into the interior of the punt well revealed three minnows left there by some other angler. One of these tempted a last fish to my basket, a three-quarter pounder, and the smallest of the three brace.

That was the end of it. I made an effort to catch sundry large roach which occasionally swam into view, but, beyond two nibbles at a bit of silkweed, got no response, and eventually departed for a very late luncheon with my seven fish, weighing nearly ten pounds. Such a basket does not often come my way in these hard times.

But the day was not yet over, and more pleasure was

in reserve. About 6 p.m. I wandered out again, armed with my biggest fly-rod, a powerful split-cane of eleven feet three inches, and ready for the evening rise. It did not begin till after eight, and then the big trout began to rove about, making great waves on the shallows. But they only came up once or twice apiece, and in the splashy way which does not mean business.

One splash, however, was close to my own bank, in a likely corner, and I waited below the spot in case the fish should come on to rise properly. In due course he did so; after trying several patterns I got a head-and-tail rise at a sedge, and then we raced down-stream together for quite one hundred and fifty yards, with intervals of leaps and cross-rushes on the fish's part. With the exception of one big fish at Blagdon, I have never had a trout on which was so suggestive of a wild salmon; the failing light and powerful rod helped the illusion. When eventually he was out and on the bank, it transpired that he, like the roach of the morning, was hooked in the pectoral fin. He weighed three pounds six ounces, and made a grand finish to what in the circumstances I shall always regard as one of the most delightful days I have ever had.

CHAPTER NINETEEN

The Inviolable Shade

Still nursing the unconquerable hope,
Still clutching the inviolable shade...

I have a dim memory of having read somewhere that Matthew Arnold was a fisherman in his lighter moments. Whether that be so or not, he could not have turned two lines more aptly to my purpose. For three full weeks have I been nursing the unconquerable hope; for three full weeks have I been clutching the inviolable shade; and now I hereby retract all that I have said upon the subject, and make solemn recantation of my heresies. Three short weeks ago I was to be numbered among the umber's friends and apologists. I knew comparatively little of him, it is true, but that little was certainly to his advantage. The thought of him carried me back to the rippling fords of Teme, where I first made his acquaintance with great pleasure and some profit, and I regarded him as one of the jewels in the angler's crown - not so bright, perhaps, as the trout, but by all means worthy of his setting. Now, however, I know him for the knave he is, and am become his enemy. And this is the manner of the conversion.

Over the wine-cup, or the modern drinking utensil which in these degenerate days has supplanted it, we were speaking of holidays. 'There are far too many grayling there,' said the expert, insidiously, 'and you'd get the tail-end of the trout fishing.'

I hesitated; meditation had been busy with a certain unknown nook in Wessex, where the great roach are. But the expert went on persuasively: 'There are some very big grayling there.'

He spoke of two-pound fish caught in the May-fly season and returned, that they might be taken again when in condition as three-pounders. He mentioned five brace as the kind of basket that ought to be the daily reward of painstaking effort, and finally he appealed to my sense of duty. The trout were being shouldered out of the stream by their rivals, and it was incumbent on every honest man who had the good of the water at heart to do what in him lay to keep the stock of grayling within limits.

At last, after a little mental arithmetic (five brace a day for a week come to the considerable total of seventy fish, the weight being, of course, 140 lb), I allowed myself to be convinced, and said that I would go and catch these fish. Could not the expert come too? But no, the expert was obliged to keep down the stock of grayling in another river, and therefore he feared he could not manage it.

It has since occurred to me that he did not reveal the whole of the matter. I have noticed that his fine catches of grayling always come from some other river, and I have a suspicion that he knows more of the inviolable shade than appeared from his conversation. But at the time I was quite satisfied with the results of the mental arithmetic, and after laying in a large stock of the numerous 'fancies' and 'terrors', whose varied brilliancy is warranted to kill grayling in any water or weather, I started for the little Berkshire trout stream, to which I have so far rather vaguely alluded as 'there', and in a few hours was standing by its side waving a particularly vivid 'fancy' to and fro in the air, and nursing the unconquerable hope with great affection.

On the day of my arrival the trout rose, and I forgot all about keeping down the grayling, though I could see them in the water, and realised that the expert had not overstated their numbers or exaggerated their size more than is pardonable. In the evening, therefore, I found that I was short of the day's total of five brace by the total itself, though I had not done badly with the trout. I determined that this must not occur again; I had come down to catch grayling, and not trout, and grayling should be caught.

Yet, such is the value of good resolutions, the second day saw me again fishing assiduously for trout which, by the way, seemed to like the gaudy fancies and terrors used as a kind of compromise with conscience; if I was not definitely fishing for grayling I was at least using grayling flies. And so the evening again came, bringing a deficit of five brace.

Plainly, I should have to have a really big day with the grayling to balance my accounts, and on the next morning I settled down to a shoal which was found rising on the edge of a long bank of weeds. They rose well for some hours, and I nursed my unconquerable hope, and cast diligently across a rather awkward breeze. But it presently began to dawn upon me that the undertaking was not quite so easy as I had imagined. Fancies and terrors were all tried in turn, and all discarded. The dark olive dun, which was on the water in fair quantities, failed to secure a rise. Black Gnats, Red Quills, Little Marryatts, Sedges red and silver, the Red Tag itself, all seemed to be useless, and at last the unconquerable hope was, so to speak, put away into its cradle while I considered the problem.

Finally, a Wickham floated rather cynically over an obstinate fish and was taken. 'At last!' I murmured, as I hurried downstream in obedience to the grayling's peremptory demand. A good fifty yards were covered, and I saw no more of him than his great back fin once. Evidently this was one of the two-pounders taken with the Mayfly and returned that he might be retaken as a three-pounder. But, alas, hardly had I decided on the inscription that should adorn his glass case when he stopped and shook himself, and the fly came away.

For a minute or two the cradle containing the unconquerable hope was in hazard of being kicked across the meadow, but calmer counsels prevailed, and I comforted myself with the thought that if I had lost a fish I had found the fly. The Wickham was to retrieve my fortunes, and to make up the fifteen brace which were now in arrears, for the grayling rise was over for the day. The Wickham would, however, have to work hard, I reflected, as I returned to my abode.

On the fourth day this inestimable fly did its best, and I actually caught a grayling of about a pound, and lost two others - a result not particularly gratifying, but lucky for the unconquerable hope, which was in some danger of being left in its cradle permanently.

It was on the fifth day that I saw a grayling a yard long - that, at least, is the length suggested by the unconquerable hope which I was nursing, as it was early in the morning. The circumstance, however, prevented me from catching anything, for the fish in question kept me busily employed all day. I now lacked 24½ brace, and the Wickham refused to help me any more.

The sixth day saw another grayling in the basket. He

was caught by accident, for he took the olive that was meant for a rising trout. The seventh day was somewhat notable. On that day the grayling a yard long rose at a Black Gnat which I offered him. I missed him, of course, and the week ended with a deficit of 34 brace.

In the evening of the seventh day I had an argument with the unconquerable hope. 'If,' it said, 'you stay here long enough you will get another rise out of that yard-long grayling, and you may catch him.' It added also, that grayling are well known to be uncertain fish. It was possible that any day might find them feeding madly. I should be sorry to have missed the carnival. I gave way, and decided to give them another week, and then the gales began.

Each day brought high wind and a sullen sky, and the whole week added two more small grayling to the catch. I did not get another rise from the grayling a yard long.

Of the infirmity of purpose which caused me to waste a third week in clutching the inviolable shade I do not care to speak. The gales continued, and I basketed a fish on each of the two worst days. The last three were ideal days for grayling, and the fish were rising all over the river at everything, apparently, except the artificial fly, which I used in all the ways known to me, both dry and wet, with less result than one would have thought possible - seven rises in all, including one short one from the grayling a yard long.

And so at the end of the three weeks I find myself 102 brace of grayling to the bad. Trout, indeed, I caught, but I did not seek for them. I wished to keep down the stock of grayling, and I have failed lamentably. Somehow the deficit must be made good. There has been some talk of a net, a stern proceeding which in the old days I deprecated. But now I shall be very happy to lend a hand to the ropes, and the only thing that keeps my unconquerable hope alive is the possibility of being able to stamp on that grayling a yard long when he has been netted out onto the bank.

CHAPTER TWENTY

Three Wild Days in Wessex

It was hard to understand at the time why, at the natural and innocent inquiry as to his favourite bait, the local authority should suddenly shut up like some sensitive plant. He had been nobly and generously expansive, measuring his catches of fish as if they were coals, by the sack, but now he was reticent and cautious. 'Sometimes I use one thing, sometimes another,' he said. The reason for the change of attitude became clear later (when he was one day discovered in close proximity to a net) but for the present it mattered not. It was enough that he had revealed where fishing was to be had which involved the substitution of a sack for the more ordinary and modest creel, and there was no unnecessary delay in putting this important discovery to the proof. A sack, two sacks - for there were two anglers - were put into the waggonette with the tackle and lunch, and the river was reached before 10 a.m. had struck by the church clock on the hill.

It was not a promising day; summer, after two months of hopeless severity, appeared to be endeavouring to surpass itself, and leaden masses of cloud swept across the sky at the bidding of a rushing, mighty wind. But the river, seen from the high stone bridge on which we were standing, looked as attractive as the keenest seeker after free fishing would desire.

Above the bridge was a broad gravel shallow on which were doubtless the dace of which the local authority had spoken, and it might be, a trout or so as well. In the distance the mill could be seen through some trees, and a point above the shallow where the two streams met suggested a back water as well as the mill stream, and presumably a weir pool. Below the bridge the river curved away among trees in a tempting succession of stream and pool. The problem, inevitable on a new and unknown water, arose: what was to be fished for, and where? The fly seemed hopeless in such a wind, the shallows were no better than a storm-swept sea, and indeed, so far as could be seen, the water above the bridge was shelterless.

Below, a clump of trees a meadow's distance away offered more hope, and thither the indomitable companion strode firmly, without wasting words. His instinct proved to have been right; the river turned a sharp corner under the shadow of the trees, forming as perfect a pool for perch as could be met with. The rods were quickly put together, and soon two red worms were offering wriggling attractions to the fish in two convenient eddies, and the anglers sat somewhat sheltered from the icy blast.

Almost immediately the indomitable companion's float disappeared, and a fish was hooked, which turned out to be a nice perch of nearly a pound. It fought gamely, but the pool was too deep for weeds, and the net soon claimed its own, while the wind shrieked with renewed vigour, as though to celebrate the success. Incidentally it tore from a tree a piece of wood that was almost big enough to be called a branch and hurled it to the ground in dangerous proximity to the head of the indomitable companion. He however paid no attention. He calmly rebaited his hook, and was soon fast in another perch, which was also safely landed.

I had so far not had a bite and I stirred uneasily as the wind hurled down another piece of wood that was quite a branch, this time near to my own head. The indomitable one continued to catch perch, and the landing of each fish seemed to be a signal for a shower of missiles from above, which were steadily increasing in size. At last, as a great log came down with a resounding thud about a yard from me, I arose, seized my tackle and, announcing that I thought I would go on and explore upstream, departed without unnecessary delay, leaving the indomitable one in the course of extracting the hook from his sixth perch with an extremely cheerful countenance. It was long, he said, since he had had such sport.

Some hundreds of yards were covered before it was deemed safe to look back, and then, amid what Horace calls a world tottering to destruction, a bending rod showed that a seventh or, it might be, even an eighth fish was being added to the basket. A pious wish was uttered that the ruins might miss that heroic being, and then the hasty flight was resumed. Such a gale surely there was never yet on sea or land; the poplars below the bridge were bending like fly rods and creaking like a rusty winch; other more stubborn trees were being destroyed piecemeal; but in the bridge itself and its high embankment there was hope - they could hardly be blown down. And behind there was a welcome calm, in which a perturbed angler might collect his faculties, and presently, for sheer shame, I put a fly rod together. It would be possible to cast within a few yards of the embankment, and the dace might, like the perch, be on the feed, out of a spirit of pure contradiction.

And oddly enough, this proved to be the case. A pluck at one of the three flies was felt at the first cast - it was impossible to see a rise. At the second a fish fastened, and was landed without much ceremony. In such weather the finest tackle would have been a mockery and undrawn gut disposed of the dace, for all he was the half of a pound, with promptitude and despatch.

Then began such an hour of sport as may never come again. The fish seemed literally mad for the fly, and Black Gnat, Soldier Palmer and Coachman were all taken with instant impartiality; and it seemed that the dace were all big ones, running between half and three-quarters of a pound. Several times two were on the cast together, and once even three, of which one got off. Many were lost; in such a wind it could not be otherwise, for it was impossible to attempt to humour a lightly hooked fish; but the fifteen pounds of dace that had been amassed by the time the rise was over seemed to justify the sack, which they half filled.

The indomitable one, whom a merciful Providence had spared, appeared in time to assist in the counting. He had, he complained, been prevented from making a phenomenal bag of perch by the trivial circumstance of a tree being blown down into the very pool which he was fishing. As it was, he had only caught eleven, with three roach of a pound each, and the tree having disturbed the river somewhat, he had also set out to explore. Exploration was, however, interrupted by the coming of the rain, which had so far held off and the day's fishing ended prematurely. Nevertheless, as we went homewards we agreed that the local authority was a very estimable person, and that we were singularly fortunate in having stumbled on a piece of free fishing which even the English climate could not render bad. When the weather improved, we assured each other, we should do something remarkable in the history of angling; all that was necessary was a little patience until the gales should have blown themselves out. Summer cannot always disguise itself as winter and after two months we were entitled to hope for better things.

So we waited our chance and studied a depressed and unsympathetic barometer. At last one morning the wind dropped and the indomitable one greeted me at breakfast with the words, 'It's going up.' I hastened to verify this glad intelligence. Sure enough the needle had moved; it no longer presaged seismic convulsions and disheartening phenomena of that kind, as it had been doing for some weeks, but was content to indicate 'rain'. This, my companion pointed out, clearly meant a fine day, since no barometer could be expected to recover itself all in a moment from such upheavals as we had been having and any upward movement at all was a sign of complete change; now therefore was our expected opportunity. The greyness of the sky, he explained, was a sure sign of midday heat.

We started accordingly. During the drive I surveyed the heavens with suspicion, and when we reached the bridge I called his attention to a certain rumbling noise that was going on in the distance. I am always diffident about rumbling noises when I am fishing; one has read horrible stories about fire falling from heaven upon the angler, by way of his rod, and consuming him. But the indomitable one knows no panics of this kind; he said it was 'guns on Salisbury plain.' Those weapons also, in some obscure way, seemed to account for the oppressiveness of the air and the indubitable masses of heavy cloud that hung low at all points of the compass. Having explained these things, he led the way upstream to the weir pool, which we had decided to fish that day. It was a deep, still hole, with very little current coming over the sill, and to me it had a dark and dismal appearance; I never can take a cheerful view of any water when there is a rumbling noise in the distance. However, the rods were fitted together, some ground bait was thrown into the pool, and we began to fish for roach.

There were no bites and apparently no fish in the pool to cause them. Presently, too, I felt called upon to observe that the guns on Salisbury plain must be getting nearer, since the sound was steadily increasing in volume. The indomitable one suggested that a breeze was getting up and was assisting the noise to travel. But there was no breeze and, so far as I could see, no excuse for his equanimity. Before long I was compelled to ask ironically if he thought there were guns all round us, because the rumbling was now plainly coming from several directions at once and to the meanest intelligence was obvious and alarming thunder. He admitted rather regretfully that there did seem to be 'thunder about,' and after an awe-inspiring clap remarked that there must be a good storm somewhere; when it broke the fish would wake up. He had long been curious to find out whether fish really did feed well in a thunder storm. With this he threw in another handful of ground bait.

I, however, had risen when the last peal began. My interest in the scientific effect of electricity was languid. I said: 'There are three good storms and in about three minutes they will be here. I don't believe the most perverted fish would bite in three thunder storms and I shan't wait to see.' The indomitable one laughed and I fled, taking refuge in the sitting room of a little farm hard by the mill. We neither of us know to this day whether fish will bite in three thunder storms better than in one or none, because even the indomitable one was compelled to retreat before the torrential downpour that began in a few minutes and lasted until after five. The mill formed a convenient centre for three separate storms, each one more violent that the other and we spent an unprofitable day looking out of the window and watching the lightning as it played about and destroyed the surrounding country. When the rain did stop eventually the river was the colour of pea soup, and roach fishing being out of the question, we went home disconsolate.

After this the barometer needle went back to its prognostication of earthquakes and the indomitable one refused to fish any more. It was not that his heart quailed before our English summer, but it was filled with righteous indignation. A refusal to fish seemed to him the only way in which he could mark his disapproval of the weather. I acknowledged that he was right, but still I badly wanted to try the stream again, for I was certain that its possibilities were untold. So one morning I bethought me of the old adage which promises sunshine before eleven if it has been raining before seven.

It was raining nicely at half past six and a brisk wind got up about nine. There was just a chance when I started that this would dissipate the clouds and give the sun its opportunity. I took a fly rod and set out in my waders and a short mackintosh coat, determined to give the dace on the shallow another trial. The water was reached about half past ten, just when the clearing up ought to have begun, if there was any truth in adages, which there is not. As a matter of fact the rain chose that time to begin in real earnest, and continued vigorously for the rest of the day.

I endured many things, including sodden sandwiches for lunch and persevered in spite of them all. But the fish did not seem to appreciate my efforts. It may be that Wessex dace demand more violent weather than was vouchsafed to them that day. The wind, it is true, was creditable and the rain did its best, but there was no mad rise such as there had been before. The fish came short and it was not until I retired to the shelter of the bridge and added to each fly on the cast a tiny tail of white kid that I could manage to catch any at all. With that extraneous aid three dozen nice little fish, averaging perhaps three ounces, were creeled. The big ones seemed to have vanished and there was not a half pounder in the whole catch. I proved, however, to my complete dissatisfaction, that mackintosh does not make a man weather-proof. Between a short wading coat and the back of one's waders there is a small, unprotected gap; the rain finds it out immediately and one is more miserable than if one were wet all over.

There was only one bright spot among those grey, damp hours. About six in the evening a March Brown, that had been put on as tail fly for a change, rose a fish which at once leaped into the air and unmistakably proclaimed his quality and species. He ran out line in grand fashion and it was some minutes before he could be coaxed down to the net - a trout of well over a pound and a half, which in shape and condition was perfection itself. His capture formed a curious conclusion to a curious experience of weather and fishing.

CHAPTER TWENTY ONE

Four Merry Tides

' Well, he got plenty of fresh air, anyhow.' This relates to the doings of an elderly gentleman who is said to have fished for bass from the rocks for a period of weeks - or it may have been months - and who was quoted to me as an example. One bass made an uncertain appearance in the story, but whether he caught it, or saw it, or just said how much he would have liked to catch it, I am not sure. I suspect, after experience, that the third alternative is the most probable.

I am in no sense an accomplished sea angler. Circumstances have not enabled me to cast lines into the sea for years and my memories of days when I used to angle for coalfish on the north-eastern coast are growing dim. Still the prospect of a long weekend on a rock-fringed edge of Devonshire fired my ambition. I would take rods and flies and spinning baits and I would spend a merry tide or two among the school bass which, as I knew right well, always rewarded conscientious efforts in such places. The report of the elderly gentleman's doings could not depress me permanently. Perhaps he had the wrong flies. Certainly he could not have had a green spoonbait. Nobody except myself has ever held a spoonbait over a candle and turned it green by the simple process of rubbing it with green sealing wax – at least, I don't expect anybody has. So I had already a considerable advantage over the elderly gentleman. Green things appeal to sea fish. I remembered how the small coalfish of the north would hurl themselves by twos and threes upon a green lead, ignoring the more tempting spinning baits which glittered in its wake. Hence the manoeuvres with the sealing wax. Oh yes, and I would catch a pollack or so to relieve the monotony of constant bass. Pollack haunt rocks and they take spinning baits and flies. I remembered some in a still mistier past, good sporting fish which gave me vast pleasure. A few pollack, by all means.

So I travelled a long distance at huge charges (if this new association succeeds in pulling down railway fares it will earn the blessings of the angling brotherhood), and eventually found myself balanced uncertainly on the rocks which I had pictured in my imagination. They were not, however, quite the same rocks. The fretting of tireless seas had worn them into miniature gulleys, with razor-edged or needle-pointed protuberances. Of their power to damage the inexpert cragsman I still bear painful signs. The rocks which I had figured to myself must have been an aberration. After all, I suppose you hardly ever get rocks neatly finished off with concrete and furnished with comfortable sitting accommodation. I must have been dreaming of piers.

The sea surged fiercely round, about and over the ledges. As soon as I saw it I realised that my green spoon was an absurdity. If it had been a spring tide I should never have dared to throw it into that waste of waters. Impudence has its limits. As for flies, I never unpacked them. My spoon was battered about by the Atlantic for half an hour or so and lost all its green sealing wax against the rocks. Then I humbly withdrew, to some extent on all fours. But that had more to do with the uneven going than with a contrite heart.

For I was not contrite - I was annoyed and I made me a sturdy paternoster and came again at the next tide. For bait (it came back to me with a rush how difficult the bait question had always been in sea fishing, unless one laboured)

I had one tiny mullet which I found marooned in a little pool and I prised half a score of stout limpets from a rock. A poor bait your limpet, I conclude, but he has the merit of being steadfast. Nothing could get him off a hook, I am sure. A great crab tried very hard and I very nearly secured him in the act. Had not a wave meanly detached his grip just as I had him swung ashore I should have triumphed. He rolled over and over down the steep slope and I thought mournfully of dressed crab. But with half the baby mullet I had a real bite and caught a conger. Congers have deteriorated, I think. I am almost sure that they used to be more than 24 inches long when Plancus was Consul and I caught them in Fishguard Bay, before there was any railway there. Frankly, I was ashamed of my conger and returned him to the ocean. I withdrew again, even more annoyed, but less humbly. One gets accustomed to razor-edges in time.

Before the third tide I took drastic steps. At low water a shrimping net secured for me a score or two of large shrimps and small prawns which I placed in a basket with plenty of wet seaweed. I also collected mussels in quantity and so I came to the fishing better equipped. Also, I placed a big float on the line, so as to approach the bass in the style advised by the authorities. The shrimps were lively and the mussels succulent; but the fish were not interested. I had one bite of which I was sure and hauled up a small wrasse. There may have been a nibble or so beside, but I could make nothing of them. Though the sea was much calmer, the bites only just bobbed the float. I do not think it can be right to have to fish in the sea with the instantaneous striking appropriate to roach. And anyhow you cannot do it with a pike rod and float. I withdrew for a third time, carrying my wrasse. That is, they tell me, the poorest fish for eating which swims our seas. Yet one more merry tide saw me on the rocks. It blew a capful all night with the result that the Atlantic came at me mountains high. But for the outer reef, it would have finished the whole affair and doubtless me too. I had no certain bites on this occasion and the waves simply did what they liked with my tackle. But at last, after they had thrust it into a crevice, I pulled up to find something hanging on to the lower hook. I looked at it with suspicion. It was small and black and repulsive. I remembered age-old warnings. 'You are a weever, I believe,' I said to it. And I treated it as such. Subsequent research has justified me. A weever it was. Soon after, the wind and waves became too much for me and I withdrew finally.

So that is the story of my sport with bass and occasional pollack. The elderly gentleman has, I fear, the laugh of me, however badly he may have done. You might think that I had had enough of sea angling after all these tides. But no, I feel as though I had just begun, and I badly want to be at it again. The tang of the salt west wind, the irresistible rising of mighty waters, the flecks of foam scattered like down over the black rocks, the solitude undisturbed save by a wheeling gull or a cormorant flying low towards the distant estuary - it is all fascinating beyond words. Add a few silver-scaled bass or emerald-gleaming pollack and I can understand how men forsake the placid trout stream for the untameable sea.

CHAPTER TWENTY TWO

End of Season

Ihave just been out to look at the river. She rolls seaward in
fine profusion and her complexion is that of noble porter,
clear with golden lights in it as the sun strikes through to the
gravel, which makes the fisherman bless his stars and his soul
as he eagerly fashions his 'figure eight' on and through the
eye of his Silver Wilkinson.

'The fisherman' - I am precise in my description, for
there be raptures unknown to the mere tourist, or to the man
with the little brown bag who passes over the ancient two-
span bridge thinking of orders. A fisherman is a person slung
about with curious devices and oddly apparelled as to the legs
and feet. He carries what in the distance looks like a long and
tapering carriage whip and what with his disreputable, much-
enduring hat, his uncouth gait and gestures, his (occasionally)
beetling brows and darkling eye, old and nervous ladies have
been known to pause at the sight of him, to stand awhile and
gaze and then without more ado to set their best foot going at
its best pace in the opposite direction. *Probatum est*, as I must
reluctantly confess. For all that, the fisherman is a very honest
man, as has been sufficiently established by respectable
iteration.

It is this worthy individual whose heart is uplifted by
yon movement of deep dark waters. I know of no one else
who shares the joy, unless it be the painter and he would
probably, after his kind, be just as pleased with a summer-
dwindled trickle oozing through a dense growth of silkweed.
No doubt that has its interesting aspects and no doubt up-

standing boulders have well-modelled contours and high lights as well as low. The painter, poor fellow, does not know that they should not be up-standing in a river that is a river. How should he appreciate the fact that a boulder ought to peep out modestly, so that when you can just see its brow you are able to pronounce for the sand eel and presently, as its nose slowly emerges you can say 'Ah, now we can put up a fly.' Every man has his limitations. I cannot seriously blame the painter, even when he lends himself to the promulgation of heresies.

Bah! Why should I affect to be more authoritative on the subject of boulders and their meaning than any other layman? To every man his ounce of knowledge. Doubtless the fisherman is well-informed about rivers, but then I am not a fisherman. I wear clothes just like the man with the little bag - at least, their intention is the same, though their performance is somewhat handicapped by their great age - and my feet are covered with the thin leather of city dwellers. No old lady would run away from me now, I feel sure. I must look almost 'like anybody else'. Why this reversion to type?, you may ask. The answer is short and sad. The season ended yesterday.

And what a season it has been! You would never believe what a season it has been unless you had shared it. That brimming draught of porter is, I am assured, positively the first that has been vouchsafed to thirsty souls since the early summer. And now it comes too late to appease their cravings. The first flood of the season fines into order as the clock strikes for close time! It is as ironic a situation as ever I met with. For two pence I would - but no. Several people whom I esteem play the game with funny clubs. Let me not libel it as a mere expedient for manifesting rage. Probably it has merits, and anyway I expect I shall be fishing again next year, so it is no good uttering rash oaths.

End Of Season

A certain number of fish had crept up to the lower reaches from the tideway when I got there three weeks ago (the railway strike delayed my starting, as it delayed so many more important projects) and for a fortnight I angled assiduously with the shrimp, which I have gradually come to regard as the only lure worth much in low clear water. It is worth more (this is a new piece of knowledge) in its natural brown dress than when 'clothe'd all in green-o,' as the song has it. Salmon must get quite enough silkweed in the natural course of a drought without seeking it in little dollops which jump strangely up and down in mid or lower water. It may be that I should have fared better in sport if my shrimp had less frequently been obscured from view in this way. It is certain that I should have given the Recording Angel less to do. So nearly everybody would have gained - there was a great collection of people to whom I had proposed little tokens of esteem in the shape of salmon flesh in pounds or in the best event, in kilos. They go hungry, the Recording Angel busy and I sorry. It is a bad world.

I have two fish to my score and two only. Both took a shrimp and they weighed respectively a little over 10 lb and 12 lb. The only notable feature about either capture was that I got the bigger one on a stiff little trout rod of 10 ft 6 in, and killed it in less time and with greater ease than the other, which was played with a light 16 ft. A short rod handles a big fish pretty masterfully provided it has some backbone and provided that the gut is strong. Those thrilling battles of the chroniclers have never come my way, but then I have never hooked a salmon on very fine gut.

The art of shrimping when I first knew the river was mostly a species of dibbling such as Izaak Walton practised for chub, save only that the lure worked below the surface, instead of on it. The angler behaved otherwise in much the same manner as Walton, hiding behind bushes, balancing himself on projecting tree trunks (an admirable feat) and otherwise concealing his presence. The salmon - but it took me a longish time to learn how the salmon behaved. The first season or two I only became familiar with the ways of rocks which are crude, even brutal. Later I had better luck and even saw fish take my shrimp. Once I remember, I had a grand view of a fine big fish poised a foot or two below the surface quite close to me. I watched him with much interest, wondering how he came to be there and what he was doing. And after a longish time I distinctly saw him eject something from his mouth - my shrimp, or what was left of it, to be precise. That taught me something.

Nowadays the dibblers seen to be outnumbered by the casters. I saw some extremely pretty fishing by several experts who were able to cast their shrimps with a gravamen of lead wire on the mount or trace as much as twenty-five or thirty yards and that from the reel, which is uncommonly good work. Personally, I got one of my fish by casting (a dressed line coiled on the hand, Thames fashion, being my method) and the other by a sort of flyfishing action which I have liked to use where it is possible. But you want to be very canny about the back cast with a shrimp, or it comes to speedy grief. Undoubtedly, however, the casting from a reel is the most efficient plan and having acquired the necessary engine, I intend to practise till I can master the art.

One of the brightest incidents in my holiday was this. A very excellent angler was good enough to ask my advice. There was a bit of a breeze and he proposed a fly. Thoroughly flattered, I said, 'Hm! Ha! Well, I think in this light and with the water as it is, I should try a Thunder and Lightning about three-quarters of an inch. Get in by that tree and if he takes, it will be about there.' I had about as much real faith in a fly as I should have in a top hat or a copper kettle, but I wore my optimistic manner and to my astonishment 'about there' a fish did take and presently I had the pleasure of gaffing it, a nice little grilse of some 6 lb or more. And I learnt that though he had caught many a trout this was the angler's first salmon, which made the incident the more satisfactory. Even now I feel a glow of undeserved pride.

After all this shrimping and vexation came the expected debacle. The glass fell, the wind howled, rain became hail, softened to snow, resumed its proper consistency and the flood began. The first part was unspeakably dirty and leaves came down in an almost solid mass. The next was hardly better, while the next saw the season out. And so it is numbered with the past. Were it not for the conventions of history I should say that it was not worth numbering. It has been, and that is all about it.

CHAPTER TWENTY THREE

Fisherman Billy

' As long as my boat,' says Old Billy firmly, looking with pride upon the great pool at our feet. We have been speaking of certain legendary carp that lend romance to the place. Old Billy, it appears, has from time to time seen a colossal tail threshing the surface, and he will not permit himself to estimate the weight of the body to which it belongs. Old Billy is one of those grandly untruthful persons who will not occupy themselves with the smaller statistics at all. The carp are undoubtedly there; they are numerous; and they are as long as Old Billy's boat: that is the thread of his discourse unravelled from the tangle of metaphor and illustration. 'You can't catch 'em,' is his impolite conclusion; 'nor can nobody,' is his afterthought, dictated probably from interested motives, for have I not on sundry occasions given the old villain the wherewithal to buy beer? Even Old Billy recognises the unwisdom of particular charges of inefficiency against the person who, for the time being, represents a day's wage of unknown quantity.

However, I am not prepared to quarrel with his assertion, partly because I have never been able of set purpose to catch carp anywhere, and partly because I am not quite convinced that these particular carp have existence other than theoretical. Twice have I been within measurable distance of belief - once when fishing for bream with a bunch of larvae of blue-bottles (politely known as gentles, impolitely known as maggots), and I hooked something irresistible which ran out all the line and destroyed it at leisure in the depths; once again, when a stout new salmon cast parted like cotton on the strike. But these events are of the now distant past, and time has induced wiser incredulity; probably in both cases I hooked a pike, a circumstance that often precedes angling misfortune.

On this sharp winter morning it is somewhat out of place to speak of carp and, but for Old Billy, I should not have done so, for we are intent on pike, and pike only. Old Billy, however, must always ease his mind on the subject; in some obscure way he seems to think his own credit and reputation greatly increased by the presence in the pool of fish which are enormous and uncatchable; possibly, too, he has some unrecognised vein of poetry in him which finds vent in frequent allusion to the wonders of the deep. Having dismissed the carp, however, he brings the punt round to the landing stage without further delay, and points with pride to the live-bait in the bucket; finer live-bait, he says, you could not see anywhere; money, in fact, could not buy them. Conceding the point as one which hardly demands emphasis (for Old Billy caught the live bait himself, and I have fished with him before), I get into the punt and instruct him to push off.

The pool is some eighty yards in width and some hundred and twenty in length, and it is in parts very deep - bottomless, according to Old Billy. The great river which forms it here plunges over weir-beams for the last time before it joins a river still greater a mile lower down, and it celebrates its last victory over the obstacles opposed to it by man in a fine turmoil of foam. Then the main current sweeps grandly across the pool to its channel below, leaving behind it two enormous eddies, one on each side. A finer pool for pike fishing it would be impossible to conceive; the bottom is all gravel, and the supply of fish seems inexhaustible. No matter how many may be caught one day, the next finds the pool restocked, for it is the Mecca of all the pike in many miles of the parent river.

Of this fact Old Billy is well aware, and he regards the fish from a base, matter-of-fact point of view; his avowed object is always to kill as many as he can. That is why he desired me to fish with trimmers today, a suggestion which I sternly put away. Trimmers are, in the first place, an abomination. In the second place, they are large discs of cork painted on the one side white and on the other red; a stick runs through them, and a line is wound round them, and they are sent out with a live-bait to fish by themselves with the white side uppermost. When a pike takes the bait the trimmer turns over and turns red - blushes for shame, in fact; then you go and chase it in a boat. The use of these things is reprehensible, but - no, on second thoughts I will not speak of the fascination of the game; I will merely denounce them and so leave them.

In his heart Old Billy despises me for sticking to the rod as good sportsmen ought; but fish, he admits, we shall probably catch, for both water and weather are right. There were a few degrees of frost last night and it is still cold. The amiable red sun that is now well up will make it a little less cold presently, but not much; this December day he is more

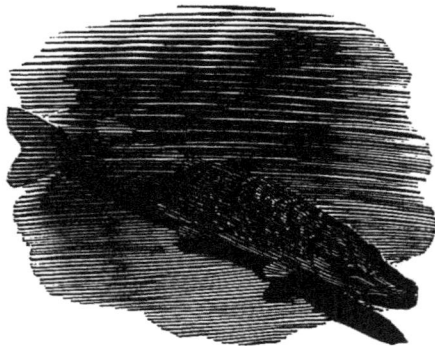

ornament than use. The air, however, is dry, and there is no wind; this is the cold that makes one vigorous and does not induce shivering fits. It is, in short, as fair a day for winter fishing as could be wished. Old Billy paddles the punt out to the marks, if I may borrow a term from those that go down to the sea in ships, and sticks in his rypecks just at the head of the farther eddy. For some unexplained reason most of the pike inhabit this part of the pool; it may be that the other eddy has less movement, and consequently has accumulated a little mud. At any rate nine-tenths of the pike taken in the pool are hooked in this eddy, and here we accordingly fish.

I have a somewhat childish liking for a beautiful float, and the one I mean to use is large and fat, its upper part a rich crimson, and its lower a deep green. I am well aware that it is conspicuous, and that the complete angler would be ashamed to attach a thing so monstrous to his line. Yet it is not so large as a trimmer, and its ruddy and cheerful countenance always seems emblematic of hope, even when the fish are least in the humour.

Equally ruddy and cheerful are the three little pilot floats which are fastened above the other at intervals of eighteen inches. They are used ostensibly to keep the line from sinking, but really for aesthetic effect; the line will not sink because it has been well greased in the manner known to dry fly fishermen, but the floats look pretty as they follow the big one in an obedient row. If the rod were long enough I should use more. Old Billy would not understand my refined pleasure in these minute things, so I do not trouble to explain them to him; instead I dangle the snap tackle before him, that he may put on a dace from the bucket.

While the floats are travelling down the eddy I have leisure to consider his appearance with more care. He is a very small man and extremely ancient, clean-shaven, and with a face wrinkled like a winter apple; yet, small, ancient, and wrinkled though he be, he can paddle a heavy boat against a strong stream, can lend a hand with the seines when the salmon are running up from the sea, can pull up his eel traps (no mean test of strength), and can carry a bucket full of water or fish as well as many a younger man. He is an astonishing example of what an open-air life will do for a sound constitution. He will never see seventy again, though his age is a matter of speculation merely; he himself is not informed on the point. So far as I can ascertain, his principal article of nutrition is beer, and though he does not stint himself therein, one would hardly think it a wholesome form of diet. Yet here he sits, this cold day, clad only in his blue jersey, patched trousers, and rubber boots, as hale and hearty as can be.

Only once have I known him to be ill. I met him outside his favourite house of call looking thoughtful and somewhat troubled. Questioned as to the reason of his dejection, he complained somewhat bitterly that the doctor had knocked him off his beer. I inquired why, and Old Billy said that the doctor had called it pneumonia; had prescribed bed and simple fare, and generally trampled heedlessly on all the patient's convictions. He had even said that Old Billy would die if he did not obey orders. I strongly advised him to fall in with the doctor's views if he could see his way to do so, and to soften the unpleasing counsel gave him something for luxuries. He said he would think about it, and as soon as I was out of sight proceeded to do so - in the public house. He consumed a regal quantity of his favourite beverage, and apparently drove out the pneumonia. Since then he has had the poorest opinion of the medical profession.

'He's under, master' says Old Billy suddenly, recalling me from my scrutiny of himself. Sure enough the big float has disappeared, and the pilots are also vanishing one by one. I wind in the slack line and tighten on the fish, which I can tell at once is only a small one. He fights gamely enough for his size, but a two-pound jack is quickly mastered, and very soon he is over Old Billy's great landing net and lifted into the punt. The hooks are taken out without trouble, and I examine them to see that they have taken no hurt from the jack's sharp teeth; suddenly I hear a sound of thumping, and looking up find that Old Billy is beating the unhappy little fish on the head with a bottle, the instrument he commonly employs for dispatching pike. This is annoying; I fully intended to put the little fellow back, for he is two pounds short of the size which I consider adequate. This I explain with vigour, and command the miscreant to release his prey and return it to the water. Old Billy gives a final decisive blow, and then, regarding the inanimate corpse with satisfaction, observes that it is too late.

He has a theory that it is fatal to success to return the first fish of the day, however small; this he explains at length, giving instances of the lamentable results of such weakness that have come under his notice. His practice, I regret to say, is to kill the small fish that come later in the day also. I have seen him in the proud possession of dead pike that could not have weighed a single pound. Mindful of this I give him very solemn warning of what will happen if he does it again, and then turn to the fishing.

Presently there is another run which results in the capture of a second pike of small dimensions; this is rescued from the bottle with difficulty. Then for a full hour the float works round and round the eddy, down the main stream, and even round the other eddy, without a touch. Old Billy snorts, and reminds me that he prophesied as much when I returned the second fish of the day; it is peculiarly unlucky to return the second fish of the day. It certainly does look as though something was wrong; it is now near midday, and two runs from little fish are all I can boast of. Moreover, there is no time to waste. It will be dark by four, and if I am to show anything like a decent basket I must work for it. Requesting Old Billy to modify his croaking, I reel in and take off the floats and snap tackle, replacing them by a spinning-trace weighted with a heavy lead.

My companion pours scorn on the idea of spinning; I shall catch nothing thus; I might possibly have caught something worth having with live bait if that fish had not been returned; as it is I shall catch nothing anyhow. The idea seems to fill Old Billy with melancholy pleasure in spite of the fact that there is a price on the head of every pike over five pounds killed by me this day. The old man is often like this: if the mood seizes him he will not prophesy good concerning his clients, but evil. I ascribe this to his having once found a dead human body in the river, a proud occurrence, which is one of the land-marks of his life. Whenever he thinks of it he becomes solemn and prophesies evil in a tone of befitting seriousness.

Afterwards he will, if allowed, relate the incident, dwelling with unction on the more gruesome details. I do not encourage the charnel-house talk, however, but request him to put a bait on the spinning-flight for me. This he does extremely well, in spite of his contempt for my policy; many decades of wicked life have taught him all there is to know about catching fish, and he is unrivalled at getting the perfect curve on a spinning-bait, an art that many fishermen never acquire at all. Practice will not do it alone; an unerring hand is needed as one of Nature's gifts, and you must arrange the hooks right instinctively at the first attempt or your trouble will be vain; there can be no revision of your work, or you will destroy both bait and temper, and in the end produce nothing better than an unseemly wobble.

Old Billy's bait spins beautifully, as can be seen by trying it close to the boat with a short line. Now I pull about thirty yards of line off the reel and coil it on the floor of the punt with some care, so that there shall be no kinking. Kinking is one of the curses of the pike fisher's lot, but with reasonable precaution it can be avoided; when one is in a boat one ought never to be troubled with it. The principal things to ensure are a clear space for the coils of line, well away from rowlocks, oars and other hindrances, a sufficiency of swivels on the trace, and last and most important, some power of self-restraint; the bait must be swung and not hurled. Swing it quite gently and it will travel an immense distance by its own weight, picking the line up cleanly and gradually as it goes. My thirty yards of line run out without let or hindrance, and then, after giving the bait a second or two to sink nearly to the bottom, I begin to draw it in, working it slowly with the rod between each draw of the left hand. In deep water one can hardly spin too slowly. Old Billy watches with a cynical eye. Mr Jones, he observes, can throw his bait fifty or sixty yards. Evidently the dead body is still in his mind, and the tribute to Mr Jones is not so important as it might seem. If the positions were reversed and I was in the counting house while Mr Jones was in the punt, I doubt not that the fifty or sixty yards would be placed to my credit.

Thirty yards are sufficient for the day at any rate. Before the bait has travelled ten it is checked, and I have that supreme sensation which makes spinning for pike so fascinating, the sensation of being in contact with some mysterious power in the depths. It is not in the least like the sudden plunge of a large trout; the feeling for the first second or two is as though the river bed had suddenly become animate and had grasped the bait in firm hands. A kind of electric thrill is communicated from the fish to the fisherman, and informs him at once that he is not fast in stump or weed; occasionally, it is true, he may for an instant think that a weed is a fish, but the real thing is never to be mistaken.

After the first few seconds of resistance the pike begins to realise his predicament, and he fights in sullen wrath. For quite a long time I cannot recover any line, and even have to concede some yards as he bores steadily out into the strong current. The firm strain tells, however, at last and I get him after several rushes nearly up to the boat, till his olive back is visible about three feet below the surface. The sight of the punt, however, rouses him to new efforts; down he goes again with tremendous power, and is under us before I can realise it. In a second he will round one of the rypecks and free as water.

In these circumstances there is but one thing to do: I plunge the point of the rod down into the water and hold him as hard as I possibly can. Now he must either break or yield, and fortunately he chooses, or cannot but choose, to yield. He is brought back to the right side, the net is under him in an instant, and he is in the boat, as pretty a seven-pounder as could be seen in a year's fishing. He is short and thick, his olive sides touched with a hint of yellow, a typical winter pike; he will eat, I give my word for it, as well as any spring salmon. He has taken a minute for each of his seven pounds to land, which gives some idea of his fighting qualities.

It has been my experience that pike of between seven and ten pounds often give more sport than far heavier fish. They play with more dash, as a rule. A big pike seems to make the error, not unknown among big nations, of underrating the forces opposed to him; but he has not the advantage possessed by them of being able to learn from his mistakes. Old Billy has by now used bottle with effect, and is looking at me without guile. 'Didn't I say as you'd catch something, master?' he demands. The incident of the dead body has faded from his memory, and he is sanguine once more.

The next thought is luncheon, which we must consume in haste, for only another hour or two of daylight remain, and I hope to catch at least another brace of fish. Old Billy declines to trifle with sandwiches; he has obeyed my instructions to provide himself with what he needs, and he indicates the half-gallon jar which is his constant companion on fishing excursions. I am glad to see, however, that he has also brought some bread and cheese.

While we eat he relates various marvels that he has seen and known. His favourite story is of the enthusiastic fisherman and the great pike which was supposed to have its home in the river above the weir. The usual way of fishing the river is to trail a spinning-bait forty or fifty yards behind a boat, and in the course of a day five or six miles of water will be covered twice. The great pike in question was said to live in a deep reed-lined reach about four miles away, and was estimated at twenty pounds.

Well, one day Old Billy was rowing the boat with two fishermen in it who had made up their minds to catch the big one. The weather was just right; the baits were all that could be wished; all things were favourable. As the boat approached the monster's haunt all hearts beat more quickly, and when, just in the right place, one of the rods bent to a heavy weight the excitement was intense.

Backwards and forwards across the river surged the fish, fighting with great power, though not with the dash of a salmon, and all three were convinced that they had got him at last. Old Billy is of the opinion that it was some hours before they got the enemy up to the boat, but that is probably an exaggeration. Up to the boat they got it eventually, however, and even then it could not be seen, nor could the angler force it to the surface.

Old Billy fortunately had his biggest landing net, a monstrous thing four feet in diameter, with a long pole as handle, and he determined to try and scoop the fish out. To his joy he succeeded in netting it and then the united efforts of the three were brought to bear and they lifted out - an enormous fish kettle. The utensil had been caught in the handle by one of the triangles, and had naturally offered great resistance to the rod, swinging from side to side in the current in the most lifelike way. If the angler had not been using the strongest of tackle he would never have landed it. Even Old Billy was deceived, he admits; and he even went so far as to look for the fish inside the kettle, but it was not there.

By this time we have made an end of eating and I begin to fish again. But curiously enough the spinning dace attracts no more pike to the net, though I get one half-hearted run from a small fish which just touches the bait and leaves it. A precious hour is spent in vain, and I can see that Old Billy's mind, for lack of occupation, is travelling back to the dead body once more. Soon he will begin to croak. This must be averted somehow and I try a new device which has often served me well in this pool before. Taking off the gimp trace I replace it by another of stout gut, and attach thereto a Devon minnow of a nondescript yellow colouring and two and a half inches long. Old Billy of course protests, assuring me that 'them things is no good,' but perseverance is at once justified, for I get a nice five-pound fish at the second cast.

Thereupon Old Billy asks me again to remember that he said I should catch fish today. Before very long I am fast in another, which is also safely landed, but which has unfortunately played havoc with the bait. The sharp teeth have practically destroyed the dressing of the hooks, and it would not be safe to trust the chances of a third encounter. I have not another Devon of the right size and colour in my box, so a spoon-bait is put on for the last half hour, greatly to the dissatisfaction of Old Billy, who has no sort of belief in spoon baits. This time he may be right, for I only catch one three pound fish, which I return hastily before he can get at it with the bottle. By now it is freezing again and the sun has set, so I decide that we have had enough. Old Billy pulls up his rypecks and we return to the landing stage.

We have a brace and a half of decent fish to show, so we have not done so badly. Old Billy disregards the forms of thanksgiving as I hand him his day's wage and something over, but again begs me to remember that he said I should catch fish. I should, he adds, have caught more if I had not returned the small ones. With that he packs four pike for me into the long rush basket and hastens away to the Black Swan, while I walk off in the opposite direction. This evening he will describe to an admiring and credulous audience the complete failure that attended my efforts until he himself grasped the rod and showed me how it should be done. By closing time he will have caught all the six fish that entered the landing net this day. But I forgive Old Billy his little weaknesses. The only complaint I would make about him is that his company has made a short winter day seem still shorter.

CHAPTER TWENTY FOUR

Blanks and all About Them

I am sorry to say that my fishing diary is no longer the candid document it was once. This sort of entry very seldom appears in it now: '19th. Fairly fine day. Cold. Blizzards. Hatch (three olives) came on at 12.45. All over by 12.47. Chucked and chanced all the afternoon. Pretty certain rose sizeable fish in Blindman's Hatch when chancing (March Brown) at 4 p.m. Return 7 p.m. train. Flies. Olive. March Brown.' Time was when I wrote that, or words to that effect, on page after page of the small green volume which contains my fishing confessions. And so each year added a fair quantity of manuscript to what will some day, I suppose, be my 'literary remains.'

But now the work hardly progresses at all, for somehow I have got into the 'Nulla dies sine pisce' habit, or - since that description might mislead - my motto is, like that of the sundial, 'Horas non numero nisi pisciferas.' How it happened I do not rightly remember. Probably by laziness. I expect I omitted to make mention at the time of some empty day, meaning just to inscribe later, '13th. Blank,' or some such little memorial of it. And as time passed perhaps I could not remember whether it was the 13th or the 12th, or perhaps the 14th and so it occurred to me that it did not matter. And so the day did not get mentioned at all.

Afterwards, I must have gradually grown to my present attitude towards blank days, which is one of contempt closely bordering on aversion. In fact, I will have no more to do with them than I can help. They have done me what harm they can. In return I will do them what harm I can. At any rate, they shall not go down into history by my aid. They shall not rank with Black Monday, Red Tuesday, St Bartholomew, Guy Fawkes, June the Fourth and all the other days of spacious memory and romantic association. 'There were days. They are dead.' That shall be their only epitaph.

I feel specially inclined to be severe on blank days just now because they have become so much more numerous of late. It is not the war. True, one has not fished much since war began, nor has one fished with the old enthusiasm and the will to succeed which goes some way towards filling baskets. But that in itself would not explain a feeling that grows upon me as to the impossibility of ever catching fishes in reasonable quantities again. Blank days must have been crowding on me for some time before August, 1914. As, indeed, the diary shows to be the case. The paucity of entries cannot by any means represent the number of occasions on which I must have started out rod in hand.

There are blanks and blanks, 'blankety blanks,' as I have heard certain intemperate persons call them. Blanks positive, blanks comparative and blanks superlative, might be another method of distinguishing them. Everyone knows the blank positive. It is just a state of fishlessness. You went out, you waited watchfully a while, maybe later you did a bit of flogging 'for warmth's sake,' as you told yourself. There was an east wind. It probably was in April, very likely on the first of the month. The water was pleasantly clear, but looked abominably cold. Entomological enthusiasm was mildly stirred by two of those yellowish brown flies which were blown riverwards from traces of cow. You satisfied your taste for botany by assuring yourself that the primroses were not yet out. The naturalist in you noted the dabblings of frogs, thus incidentally disappointing the fisherman, who is in you too, and who had hoped that the said dabblings were the risings of trout. You may have seen one or two small trout on the shallows, or in carriers, but you found nothing of respectable size in any position which suggested an intention of feeding. Indeed, the river seemed to be very poorly stocked, possibly to have suffered from serious pollutions or nefarious doings with nets. In the end you went home completely disillusioned and the day is not recorded in your diary.

The blank comparative is not necessarily devoid of fish. It may even yield a brace or a leash and still deserve all the invective that you like to cast upon it. It happens when you have an invitation to that very special piece of water, the thought of which causes your acquaintances to look at you with round eyes and say: 'By Jove, you ought to do well there. Jiggins had a day there last year and he told me...'

You do not, of course, need the testimony of the estimable, if incompetent, Jiggins to convince yourself that you are in luck's way. You know perfectly well that you are to have exceptional sport and you have been fighting its battles over in advance any time these three weeks. You have decided to do the sporting thing, though, and not kill any inordinate number of fish. Four brace will be enough, or perhaps five brace, if the water really seems to be almost too well stocked, as is not improbable. Yes, perhaps five brace. Double figures give a certain completeness to a remarkable day and, when you come to think of it, a water which is fished so seldom is really the better for a little judicious thinning. The balance of nature - there is always that to be considered. Yes, certainly five brace - or six.

The day so eagerly anticipated comes and you start out betimes to catch your train, or from the inn door, as the case may be. As you start you look dubiously at the sky, which is undoubtedly somewhat lowering. Lead-coloured clouds massing in all quarters of the heavens do not quite meet your views of what should be. However, it is early yet and much may happen before the serious business of the day begins. Even when you reach the water and find it appallingly clear in a lurid sort of light you still comfort yourself with the thought of what may come about by lunch time. A little steady breeze, for instance, would soon clear the sky, or perhaps the sun will come out and chase away the thundery haze which hangs over the valley like a ceiling over a room. Or perhaps a short, sharp storm will aerate the day, Meanwhile you are out to fish and you fish, realising as you do so that you had not over-estimated the quantity of trout in the water. You can see them everywhere, either furrowing away from the bank as you approach or lying motionless on the bottom further out. They are not rising, it is true, but there are certainly a great many of them. If they were rising - nay, when they shall be rising a bit later on, there will be brave doings.

The angler is a creature of splendid optimism and he is able to count on a rise just about to begin at any time of any day. Till it is positively too dark to see a big sedge at the end of a short line he is not ready to give up hope and even then he may have faith in a few casts with the said sedge out into the void where water and sky-line mingle. The dry fly man has been known to make good use of his ears and hand when his eyes have failed him. It is this optimism that keeps you going all through the day which is in question. The morning was unproductive, but the afternoon will make amends. When the afternoon has run its dreary course the early evening rise is due to begin. The barren early evening makes way for the evening proper, that time of cool airs and bold fish. Only after each in turn has brought its disappointment do you take your rod to pieces, convinced that your luck is wholly out. By no other reasoning can you account for the fact that you are going home with a brace of fish, one of them barely 1lb, the other an 18-inch specimen which weighs 1¼lb. Jiggins, that poorish performer, took away from this self-same water an epoch-making basket, whose occupants averaged 1½lb. You, whose ability - but, no matter.

The bitterest part of it, perhaps, is the shape of your larger fish. That, out of such a wealth of really desirable trout, providence should have seen fit to select for you one which favours an eel and which was too proud to fight is indeed a trial of your philosophy. Almost would you sooner have caught nothing at all than have just saved the blank in such a fashion. Absolute failure has its heroic side, when it is compared with the sordid details of the blank comparative.

The blank superlative is not lacking in heroic qualities and it is perhaps more to be welcomed as an experience than the blank comparative. But it does not do to suffer from it too often. It may lead to golf and similar errors if repeated with any frequency. To fail magnificently once in a way is all right and good for conversation but to make a habit of it is wrong. I am one of those men who have fished for salmon for a solid month without catching one. I have done this twice in different years. But that is enough. I can now take my position in the circle of the greatly unfortunate, even a distinguished position. Hardly any of them can say anything about salmon fishing that deserves greater sympathy.

There, however, I desire to stop. I have a strong prejudice against spending another month in salmon fishing without result. 'Integer Vitae' or some such observant person would begin to say, 'There must be some reason for this.' And, putting one and two together, he would arrive at the conclusion that I ought not to be allowed to go salmon fishing again or indeed to go anywhere or do anything without a keeper. I fully realise the danger and the justice of the inference, so if it ever happens to me again to be nearing the end of a month without having caught a salmon I shall sacrifice those few last days and come home. Then it will be possible to speak of the holiday as 'about a fortnight.' Lots of men come back clean from about a fortnight without having suffered anything worse than a blank positive.

The blank superlative, to reach its deepest depths, should of course be associated with losses. I once thought my greatest hour of blankness had come when I found it to be lunch time, with nine salmon hooked, played and lost since 9.30 a.m. To this day I am not sure whether I do not regret the fact that I succeeded in bringing the tenth to bank before I actually bit a sandwich. Had I lunched before making that cast maybe I should have finished the day in style and possibly lost a dozen. It is impossible to say, for as a matter of fact I killed two more in the evening and so the day cannot be included even among the minor blanks, mine at any rate. A three-salmon-day is for me exactly the opposite to a blank.

I have had superlative blanks with trout and have several times hooked and lost all the largest fish in a river. No angler can make any mistake about that sort of experience, I mean with regard to the size of the fish.

There can only be a limited number of trout exceeding 24-inch in any fishery and when you have hooked a dozen of them you are fully entitled to assume that there are no more. It is extraordinary how those monsters will 'lay for' you on what they know to be your off day. They positively gambol in your path, pretending innocent delight in smuts and other things that no 24-inch trout ever genuinely condescended to notice. Of course they know that a No. 0 hook has no power to disturb their horny-jawed complacency, while the trifling problem of either twisting it out or breaking the insufficient line jumps with their humour. And they dearly love to hear the angler uplift his voice in commination. Nowadays, if I find a 24-inch trout at the first bend, I keep my eye lifting. If there is another at the second I scan trouble and if a third greets me near the stile, I prepare my mind for the buffets of evilly-minded fortune. Had I more philosophy I would go off to the grayling shallow and ignore trout altogether. But how can a man acquire such philosophy?

Other species of blank there may be and doubtless are, triangular blanks, for instance - the sort of thing that may happen to a harler on the Tay with his three rods, if a blank ever does occur on that pompous river - or rhomboidal blanks, if our ex-President will forgive my trifling with the 'chief of sciences,' as Aeschylus called it. Perhaps he will, on account of my complete ignorance of the subject. I conceive a rhomboidal blank to be a figure representing the passage of an angler downstream when he wears trouser waders and has temporarily, or permanently, got both head and feet well submerged. While it is certainly rhomboidal, I assume this to be a species of blank.

Anyhow, a man can't be catching fish when all you can see above the surface is the seat of him. I can imagine other kinds of blank, the blank debateable, for example in which a fish of some eminence has been caught but has slithered in again or the alleged blank,which might have some connection with boundaries and other legal technicalities. I doubt not that there is also a legal blank, which might differ materially from a blank positive and a conscientious blank of which a symptom might be the hiding of a fish under the heather till the morn's morn, the morn of course being the Sabbath.

Moral blanks, attributed bitterly by the fly purist to the bait or minnow man, public blanks, experienced by three miles of fishermen in monster competitions, private blanks, which owe their privacy to the reticence of the sufferer; in short, there is hardly any sort of blank to which we are not liable.

It says a good deal for us that we go on fishing.

More great fishing reads from Merlin Unwin Books

www.merlinunwin.co.uk

The Song of the Solitary Bass Fisher
James Batty

Chalk and Cheese
Charles Hamer

Get Fishing
Allan Sefton

Nymphing: the new way
Jonathan White

Flycasting Skills
John Symonds

Trout from a Boat
Dennis Moss

Pocket Guide to Matching the Hatch
Peter Lapsley and Cyril Bennett

Pocket Guide to Fishing Knots
Step-by-Step Coarse, Sea and Game Knots
Peter Owen

GT: a Flyfisher's Guide to Giant Trevally
Peter McLeod

How to Flyfish: from newcomer to improver
John Symonds

Complete Illustrated Directory of Salmon Flies
Chris Mann

Once a Flyfisher
Laurence Catlow

The Healing Stream
Laurence Catlow

That Strange Alchemy
Laurence Catlow

Tying Flies with CDC
Leon Links

The Fisherman's Bedside Book
BB

Confessions of a Carp Fisher
BB

Canal Fishing
Dominic Garnett

Hooked on Lure Fishing
Dominic Garnett

Flyfishing for Coarse Fish
Dominic Garnett

Fishing with Emma
David Overland

The Secret Carp
Chris Yates

Falling in Again
Chris Yates

Fishing with Harry
Tony Baws

The One That Got Away
Jeremy Paxman, Max Hastings, David Steel, et al

Lightning Source UK Ltd.
Milton Keynes UK
UKHW012111080421
381676UK00001B/32

9 781913 159306